Psychic Sight

Laura LaForce

LAURA LAFORCE

Manor House

Laura Laforce

Library and Archives Canada Cataloguing in Publication

Laforce, Laura, 1966-, author
Psychic sight / Laura Laforce.

ISBN 978-1-897453-37-7 (pbk.)

1. Laforce, Laura, 1966-. 2. Psychics--Canada--Biography. 3. Mediums--Canada--Biography. I. Title.

BF1027.L34A3 2013   133.8092   C2013-902755-6

Published 2013: Manor House Publishing Inc.,
452 Cottingham Crescent, Ancaster, ON, CANADA, L9G 3V6
905-648-2193 wwww.manor-house.biz All rights reserved
Cover Design: Donovan Davie / Cover art: Shutterstock

We acknowledge the financial support of the Government of Canada through the Canada Book Fund (CBF) for our publishing activities.

By the same author: X-tending; Journey into Spirituality; Finding X. Website: www.lauralaforce.com

"TO MY LOVED ONES"

"MAY YOU EXPERIENCE AND GROW THROUGH SPIRIT IN YOUR JOURNEY OF LIFE."

ACKNOWLEDGEMENTS

I WOULD LIKE TO EXTEND A SPECIAL WARM THANK YOU TO MY FAMILY AND FRIENDS WHO SUPPORTED ME ON MY JOURNEY.

I LOVE YOU ALL. YOU'RE A FANTASTIC BUNCH OF SOULS.

CONTENTS

INTRODUCTION			5
CHAPTER	1	MY CHILDHOOD	7
CHAPTER	2	HEAVENLY BREAD	33
CHAPTER	3	SPIRIT GUIDES	38
CHAPTER	4	TRIALS AND TRIBULATIONS	51
CHAPTER	5	A MULTITUDE OF WARNINGS	72
CHAPTER	6	THE JOURNEY TO SAFETY	83
CHAPTER	7	TORMENTED	93
CHAPTER	8	THE COURTS	103
CHAPTER	9	REVELATIONS FROM SPIRIT	109
CHAPTER	10	THE CAPRI	117
CHAPTER	11	TWIST OF FATE	130
CHAPTER	12	THE GOLDEN HEART	135
CHAPTER	13	THE SERMON	139
CHAPTER	14	DEALING WITH DARKNESS	143
CHAPTER	15	SEARCH FOR MISSING GOLD	166
CHAPTER	16	SOUL MATES	169
CHAPTER	17	WHIRLWIND OF EVENTS	182
CHAPTER	18	HEALING AND MIRACLES	187
CHAPTER	19	DEATH AND DYING	199
CHAPTER	20	COMMUNICATIONS	201
CHAPTER	21	SUICIDES	209
CHAPTER	22	GHOSTS	213
CHAPTER	23	OVERWHELMED	232

INTRODUCTION

Many people are experiencing regular spiritual encounters, but are silent out of fear of being judged. The search is on for the missing pieces of the spiritual puzzle. Perhaps my experiences will reflect some of the answers you have been seeking.

Loved ones are returning to visit us from the other side. They are attempting to communicate in a variety of ways. These visits are ranging from realistic dreams to appearing physically while awake. They're souls often appear in a lit-up beam called an orb. It is common for our loved ones to drop coins, touch hair, and cause electrical disturbances to get our attention.

Déjà vu verifies specific events. Déjà vu is the sudden familiarity of a place and or situation. I've been here before or already seen this. Déjà vu confirms our life's path or map. These points of recollection verify the direction you have previously chosen.

People are having premonitions, but are unsure of how to deal with the information. Having premonitions can be overwhelming leading to anxiety. Premonitions are notifications of upcoming events. These pieces of information surface spontaneously.

Anyone is capable of having spiritual experiences, but development is a choice. This is much like acquiring the skills to play a sport. After devoting time, the results materialize.

This book was written with the intention of being able to share my personal life experiences as a psychic medium.

As a medium, I have been able to explore what is generally unseen and unknown. On a daily basis I interact with my spirit guides.

Receiving invaluable information makes living easier. I communicate with the dead. I have accompanied souls to the doorway, which leads to the other side. While witnessing these souls on their departure, I have seen angels.

Join me on my journey into spirituality and watch as events unfold.

- Laura Laforce

Chapter One

MY CHILDHOOD

My life wasn't fun, easy or magical. I faced many challenges at a young age. By four, I was the oldest of three children. My brothers, one and two years old, shared a twin-like bond. I was the loner: two's company, three's a crowd.

At four years old, I awoke in a panic. My parents were fighting again. Angry shouting and crashing penetrated the morning air. After the noise stopped, I heard nothing else. I knew something was terribly wrong. I quietly opened my parents' bedroom door, trembling with fear.

I rushed into their bedroom and faced a horrifying bloody disaster. Big bright red splotches of blood smeared the surface of their white frayed bedspread. One of the lamps laid across the top of the bed with a partially intact blood splattered damaged lampshade. The other lamp was hanging off a tilted nightstand by its cord. Bloody tissues were strewn about the room. Spots of blood speckled the grey tiled floor, but my parents were nowhere to be seen.

In distress I frantically cried out looking for my parents. My father met me in the hallway, drying his hands on a dark towel. "We're cleaning up," he told me, heading into the bathroom.

A social worker rang the doorbell after a while. My mother went somewhere with the social worker. She didn't come home for many days. I stayed home with my father and my brothers. Father told me Mom wasn't feeling well and went for help. I remember my father reading me my favorite book while she was away.

Shortly after she returned home, we moved. The house we had been living in was on the verge of being condemned. We were poor and lived on welfare.

It was, while living in the next house, I discovered I could go through walls while sleeping. At four years old, I was astral-travelling.

My parents separated shortly after we moved. My mother had a restraining order against my father. He wasn't allowed to see me any more.

At five, I recognized the difference between life and death. I came across two dead ducks while playing outside. They were lying on top of a black garbage bag. I knew they were dead. I noticed how peaceful they both looked.

Around five I could sense the energy of different people. I knew if they were good or bad without talking to them.

At six, my mother was bathing me with my youngest brother. There was a little over four years between us. Mother was sitting on the lid of the toilet seat supervising us. My brother lost his balance while grabbing a toy and slid under the water. Mother quickly grabbed him in a hurried panic. In anger, she pushed me down, holding my head under the bath water.

With my dark hair and hazel eyes, I resembled my father. Mother resented this. The following statements would often be said before Mother flew off the handle punishing me:

"You look like your father," she'd tell me.

"You're a liar just like him," she'd repeatedly tell me.

"Be glad I raised you, I never wanted a girl," she'd mutter.

I usually didn't understand why I was being disciplined. After she calmed down, she would approach me, claiming she did it because she loved me.

At seven, a strange bearded man came to the door

handing mother Christmas presents. I wasn't much of a reader but as I struggled to see whose gifts they were. I noticed my name on a gift tag. A three-letter word was printed under my name. After repeatedly sounding out the letters of the word was Dad. By then he was gone.

"Was that Dad?" I asked.

"Is he coming back? I want to see him." Mother remained silent. I was upset and started to cry. I missed him and loved him very much.

At the end of Grade Two, I brought home my final report card. Mother handed me a card, wanting me to read it to her. I sat looking at it, but couldn't read it. Minutes later she became angry. She grabbed me by the arm and led me to the door.

"I want you to walk to church and tell the priest what you did. If you don't, there will be no supper tonight."

I walked over to the church, hoping the priest would be there. I arrived at the church, the door was unlocked and I went in. The priest came out of an office area. "Little girl, why are you here?" the priest asked.

"My mother sent me to talk to you," I answered.

"Why?"

"She gave me a card thing for passing Grade Two."

"What do you mean by a card thing?"

"It is a yellow card with letters, numbers and no pictures."

"But why are you here?"

"She sent me to talk to you, because I didn't read it to her."

"Because I can't. I don't know how?"

"Tell her you talked to me and that you'll do better next time."

After returning home, Mother met me at the door.

"Did you see the priest?"

"Yes."

"What did he say?"

"To tell you I'll do better next time."

"Are you sorry?"

"Yes."

"The card I wanted you to read, was a swimming pass for passing Grade Two."

I was eight years old when I received my first big premonition. One afternoon I was playing with my best friend Kim, who lived next door.

"Laura, I'm going on holidays next week," Kim told me.

"Kim, please don't go on holidays, I'll never see you again," I warned her.

"I have to go with my parents. I promise I'll be back."

"Try to stay safe," I begged.

I was playing outside one afternoon. "Laura, come inside, I want to talk to you," Mother coldly ordered.

"Kim's dead. She drowned on holidays. They found her floating in the water. Stay away from her house and her family. They're mourning."

Right after receiving the news, I found it very hard.

I cried when mother wasn't around to see. Mother went to her funeral and brought home a memory keepsake of Kim. Seeing this paper with Kim's picture was extremely upsetting.

It was difficult to sleep at night or to eat and drink. I started to experience anxiety, I worried about drowning. I wondered if I could accidentally drown by drinking too much water or swallowing it wrong.

I silently suffered from guilt for many years. I never told anyone what I had known for a long time. I prayed to God asking for nothing bad to happen any more.

Around nine years old, I could see neighbors bringing home babies. I was playing outside after school with Eva and Fay. "Mrs. Strong is going to have a baby boy next summer," I told them.

"How do you know that?" they asked.

"I can see her carrying a baby wrapped in blue," I answered.

"She's not pregnant, Laura," piped up Fay.

"No but she's going to be. Just watch," I replied.

"How do you know the baby's not a girl?" asked Eva.

"Girls are always wrapped in pink. When I'm not supposed to know, the baby is wrapped in white," I stated.

"How do you see that?" asked Fay.

"It's like watching a TV commercial, without the sound." I said.

"Does this happen while your sleeping?" Fay asked.

"No, this happens when I'm awake."

Another afternoon we were playing outside and I blurted out:

"Poor little Christopher is going to die."

"Laura, I'm telling! That's not a nice thing to say," Fay scolded.

"But he's going to get sick and die," I stated.

Within days he was dead. He died of meningitis.

When I was ten, Mother ran out of food and money. I ate rolled oats, white sugar and water for a week for breakfast, lunch and supper. I brought a margarine container with cold oatmeal to school for lunch. The other children made fun me. This was the same week that newspaper replaced toilet paper at our house.

I was often subjected to bullying at school, because I was different from the others. I would often daydream in class. My buck teeth, clothing and lunches were often made fun of.

I was a different child. I had dyslexia and learning disabilities as a young child. I didn't read, write, or do math until I was almost ten. I remember telling a friend during a school draw that the next prize was mine. Within seconds my name was called. I received a five-dollar prize! I knew more about my classmates' unspoken life events than I did about what was being taught in class. I found their energies very distracting.

I tried to shut down this special part of me out of fear and anguish. The gift never fully went away; it was always there, just like breathing. I attended mass every Sunday and said my prayers daily.

Amelia, my mom, became a schoolteacher when I was 12.

At thirteen, I was visiting Kevin, a friend who was in the

hospital. A dying man in the same room asked for water. "Laura, can you go help Al, he needs a sip of water," Kevin said.

At first I was reluctant and uneasy due to fear. I had never seen anyone in this physical state before. Al resembled a skeleton with skin. After helping him with a couple sips of water, he quietly started talking to me and thanked me before I left.

The following day at school a weird, cold, sickening sensation went through my body. My teacher stopped the class.

"Laura, you're very pale, Are you okay?"

"Yes," I responded. I knew Al was dead.

Right after school, I headed to the hospital to verify what I already knew.

"Al's dead; he died this afternoon," Kevin informed me, as I walked into his room.

At fourteen years old, I attended the same school Mother taught at. After running into debt, she took on a second job, returning home after midnight on a regular basis. A normal day consisted of going to school, doing homework, watching my siblings, cleaning, and cooking. On the weekends I worked at McDonalds. I often corrected Mother's classroom assignments, which she was behind on.

I was a very sensitive, shy, insecure teenager, but responsible and dependable. Mother was a very moody, controlling, angry, violent person.

One evening she happened to be home, which was rare. After supper I was helping her with the dishes. She started questioning me about school. Suddenly she became irate, while I was answering her, she kicked me. For the first time in my life, I retaliated. I kicked her back. She punched me. I

13

punched her back. Next, she tripped me and pinned me to the floor, her hands wrapped tightly around my neck with both thumbs in my Adam's apple. She was choking me to the point that I couldn't breathe. I could no longer struggle. Everything in my vision went black. I silently prayed to God asking him to take me to heaven. I was on the verge of passing out when she finally let go.

"Get up! Get up now!" she demanded.

I gradually sat up, which was not fast enough for her. I was weak after what she had done to me. She picked me up by my hair and threw me into the concrete hallway wall.

After being abused for many years, I'd had enough of the fat lips, which bled, pulled hair, welts, punches, and kicks. The situation worsened as time went on. The week before, the family physician threatened to report her to Social Services, after pushing one of my siblings down the stairs during a fit of rage. I wasn't the only child she hurt (years later, I found out that my aunt mentioned her concern to my grandmother about my Mother's abusive ways towards me).

I waited until the next morning. I told the school principal what had happened. Mother was immediately paged to the office. I was sent to class.

After school my mother was in a rush.

"We have an appointment with a psychiatrist this afternoon to get you assessed. I was called down to the office this morning by the principal. My job was on the line. I denied everything. He told me to get you help. To lie about being abused is very serious."

This led to an immediate psychiatric assessment with hospitalization. During the assessment I never spoke of what happened. I didn't need anything else bad to happen to me. Ten days later I was released. Mother was told I was fine. The assessment provided didn't suit her, she wanted me medicated.

Right away, Mother attempted to find another psychiatrist, one who would listen to her.

After interviewing several doctors she found one. Now she wanted medical possibilities ruled out. She talked to the doctor without me. I sat in the waiting room picking up the negative vibes. Then I would go in to speak with him next.

"Your mother says you see things. Is this true?"

"Yes."

"Your mother says you hear sounds. Is that true?

"Yes."

"She says sometimes you get upset and cry when you feel something bad is going to happen. You complain about being cold and tasting something awful. These could be signs that something is wrong with your brain.

"Your mother wants you tested for epilepsy. You'll have to stay in the hospital for awhile. If I find something wrong with you, there is medicine to make it better."

I really wanted to tell on her, but I didn't dare. The night before the test, I wasn't allowed to sleep. In the morning my head was hooked up to electrodes. Then both sides of my jaws were frozen with a needle. Wires were inserted through my jaws to the base of my brain. I cried in pain. I could hear and feel the wires being forced through my head. Days later, the results came back as normal. Other medical tests were performed including a CT scan of my brain. Again the results were normal.

The following day, I was playing the piano at the hospital. Suddenly, I tasted cold rotting vegetation. This was the taste of death. I saw my grandpa enclosed in a circle. I called my mother to tell her to watch out for Grandpa: "Something bad is going to happen to Grandpa. He's going to die," I said.

"Your Grandfather is fine," my mother replied. "He's just come back from holidays. Goodbye."

Days later, I was released without medication. Again she was told I was fine.

Hours after I was sent home, I started to feel uneasy. The premonition of my grandfather's death started to gradually unfold throughout the evening. My grandfather was an alcoholic and he was drunk. He was out driving around, after threatening to do himself in. Many phone calls were received and placed in regards to his whereabouts. Family members were out looking for him. I knew he wasn't going to survive the night. I prayed to God to spare his soul.

In the morning, someone came over to inform mother of his passing. I hadn't heard the news, but I already knew. Right away mother burst into my bedroom with a bottle of pills and a glass of water.

"Laura, I need you to take this pill," she insisted.

"Yesterday the doctor at the hospital told you I was fine, before sending me home. He told you I didn't need to be medicated. Why are you doing this to me?"

"These are my valium pills. You need to take one of these or else," she threatened.

I held out my hand. Mother handed me a pill and the glass of water. Mother was out of it. I wondered if she had taken one of these pills herself.

"I'll be back in awhile." She stated.

I waited for her to leave my room, before throwing the pill in the garbage.

After a while she returned to my room.

"How are you feeling?" she asked.

"Fine," I answered.

"Are you a little sleepy and relaxed?" She inquired.

"Yes," I replied.

"I'm glad you took that pill, because I have bad news for you. Your grandfather is dead. He returned home last night, pulled his car into the garage, shut the door and left his car running. He died of asphyxiation.

A couple of days later, we arrived at the funeral home.

"We're going to go into a special room to say goodbye to Grandpa." she instructed.

"I've already seen him dead, before he died. I don't want to see him. Please don't make me see him. That's not how I want to remember him."

She was livid. After finding out where he was, she came back for me. I was physically forced by her into the viewing room with Grandpa's open casket. I stood there mortified, sickened as I viewed his lifeless body.

"Touch his hand and tell him you love him," she ordered.

"No, I don't want to. He doesn't look like he did when he was alive," I insisted.

She grabbed my hand and put it on his freezing cold hands, which were clasped above his waist. I almost vomited. Couldn't she just beat me instead? I silently thought.

"Tell him goodbye," she barked.

"Goodbye," I said while sobbing with fear and sadness.

"Kiss him," she demanded.

"No," I replied.

"Kiss him," she repeated, as she grabbed the back of my head, neck and shoulders forcing me down toward him.

Being upset and uneasy, I lost my balance and fell on him. She grabbed my long hair and led me to his forehead. My lips touched his cold tight forehead and the smell of formaldehyde sickened me. I felt like I was going to pass out. Seconds later, she finally let go of me.

Weeks later, she found a psychiatrist who labeled me schizophrenic and medicated me. My mother asked him about having me sterilized. Shortly after that diagnosis, mother brought me to a healing service at the church. She told the man in charge that I was possessed and suffering from a mental illness.

Many weeks later that psychiatrist died. Mother insisted that we attend his funeral together. She wanted me to see his body, but I refused. Thankfully there were many people around. She couldn't force me to do anything.

Weeks later she found another psychiatrist. He didn't agree with the previous label, instead I was labeled bi-polar. I was medicated with something different. Shortly after, I became a ward of the government and lived in a group home.

I was medicated against my will on a daily basis. I often felt sick and dizzy.

A strict daily routine was followed. Living quarters were cleaned daily, upon returning for the day. Every second day we would sit around a dining room table and work on our correspondence for an hour. Every night after supper, one person would be chosen to scrub the kitchen floor by hand.

On the last day of every month, we were issued one roll of

toilet paper and a bus pass. A five-dollar bill was given to purchase personal effects such as pads.

One morning, I was so groggy that I didn't shower before leaving for the program. After returning, I climbed into the shower. The worker in charge immediately turned off the hot water supply. I realized what was happening but I continued to shower. I was approached by the worker on the way to the kitchen table.

"You won't be eating with the others tonight. You're dirty. You'll eat in the mudroom, on the floor with the dog."

"I just took a cold shower," I replied.

"You didn't have a shower this morning. You're only allowed to shower in the morning."

"I was tired and feeling sick," I said.

The worker handed me my supper and led me to the mudroom. At first this was upsetting. The dog and I ate supper together. It was the best supper I'd had had in years!

Several nights later, I had a severe drug reaction. I was rushed into the emergency room and immediately given a drug to counter the reaction.

I attended a daily program for troubled teens, which lacked proper schooling. English and math courses were made available through correspondence only. The greater part of my day was usually spent in a so-called therapeutic group. The group discussions were generally silly, fruitless, unintelligent and based on sexual topics. The leading therapist would come into the room and take a seat.

"What would you like to discuss today?" Peter the therapist asked the group.

"Sex," the group would always answer.

The program offered a designated smoking room/lunch room. Every lunch hour or break was spent in this smoke filled room. Being a non-smoker and severely allergic to smoke didn't help. One time I bit into my sandwich to discover someone had filled it with cigarette ashes.

A handful of teenagers were struggling with mental illness. They were treated badly and abused by the bullies on a daily basis, behind the backs of the staff. A couple of us were misplaced. Most of the kids were young offenders.

I would often be bullied into handing over my clothes or any personal possession they desired. Some of these teenagers resented me. They considered me a goody two-shoes for two reasons; I was a virgin and had never smoked drugs. I wasn't one of them.

One day after returning from the program, I was invited for the first time to join two of the four girls that I lived with in the group home. Being lonely, I accepted the invitation. Within minutes, I joined Lois and Jennifer in their room. They quickly shut the door and secured it with a dresser.

"You need to prove you're worth having as a friend through our initiation. We thought about bursting your cherry today, but we'll spare you that," Lois said.

"Laura, you're to sit in this chair and let us do your hair. You won't be able to look until were done," Jennifer ordered.

Lois and Jennifer were giggling excessively as they did my hair. I sat quietly hoping they wouldn't hurt me. About half an hour later they finished.

"Laura, we're going to let you take a look at your new hairdo, but you're not to tell on us if you don't like it," Lois said.

Jennifer handed me a mirror. I took a quick glance at my

shocking new appearance. Of all things I had a Mohawk to contend with. Thank God hair grows!

"How do you like it?" asked Jennifer. "Cool!" I responded.

The following week, a visit was scheduled with Mother. I didn't look forward to seeing her, especially not this time. I stepped into the office where teens visited their parents, always accompanied by a staff member. Mother's jaw dropped the moment she saw me. Right away she demanded that the ridiculous cut be removed and my head be shaved.

"Why did you do this?" Mother asked. "Because," I answered. The following day I was taken to a salon and where the remaining hair was shaved off. The huge earrings I had would compliment this newest style.

Shortly after turning sixteen, while I was in the program, two of my roommates jumped me and tried to choke me. They were pulled off by staff and hauled to a lock-up facility by police.

A few months before my eighteenth birthday, I'd had enough. Earlier that day I was sent on an outing with my roommate. We were supposed to shop for groceries for a special dinner for the group. She met up with her pimp and introduced me. I didn't want anything to do with these people.

The following morning, I packed an extra change of clothes in my big purse. I walked out the door and never returned. I hitchhiked to the west coast. I stayed with a couple of different families and looked for work.

One afternoon, I called a help wanted ad. There was a position for a babysitter/restaurant kitchen helper. The man who answered the phone arranged for an immediate interview. Within hours, I arrived at a brand new empty restaurant. The man opened the door to let me in and locked it behind me. I pulled out his application form and he interviewed me.

21

"Would you like to see the kitchen?" he asked.

"Yes," I replied.

As soon as I entered the kitchen he physically forced and restrained me against the counter. He terrified me, while ripping open my high neck blouse. I could hear the material give and a button hit the floor.

"I thought you said you're healthy!" he said in an angry voice. "There are zits on your chest."

He went on to assault me. I detached from my body. I wasn't able to fight him. After he left the room I tried to pull myself together. This bastard had ejaculated on my leg. I was sickened and on the verge of vomiting. I cleaned my leg with my knee high socks and stuffed them in my pocket. I wanted to go to the police, but I couldn't. I was a missing person under the age of eighteen.

A couple of days later I found a job. I was to start the following Monday. The people I was staying with went to Social Services, looking for extra funds and clothing to help me out. As soon as my name was entered into their computer, I came up as a missing person.

Soon after, two police cars showed up at the home where I was staying. I was apprehended, handcuffed and put in the back of a police cruiser. I sat silently as the cruiser left the curb. I felt angry and humiliated, being treated like a damn criminal. I'd never been in cuffs before. I looked down at my lap and the handcuffs, which now embraced my wrists like big ugly bracelets. Being double-jointed, I managed to slide my thumb through a cuff, followed by the rest of my hand.

"Guess what?" I said, while proudly swinging the empty cuff in the rear view mirror, like a lasso.

"I'd get that cuff back on pretty damn quick, if I were you. If

I have to stop this car and pull over, you'll be sorry. Those cuffs can be tightened to the point it hurts," he said.
I quickly slipped the cuff back on. I didn't want that to happen.

"When we get to the county jail, you're not to run off on us, because I'll shoot."

"You must be the bastard of the year," I said.

"I'd shut your mouth, if I were you. I wouldn't hesitate to pull over and spank you."

We finally arrived at the county jail. I was led into an office by the two male officers. A female officer working behind a tall counter was filling out paper work. My purse was handed to her by one of the arresting officers.

"I need you to take off your socks and shoes," she ordered.

"I'm keeping them until you leave."
The prison guard arrived at the office to escort me to my cell. Electronically operated barred doors opened and shut, as he led me through the facility to my destination.

My first night in the slammer was quite shocking. My cell was equipped with a metal bed which hung from the back wall by heavy chains; it was covered with a thin mattress. An ugly stainless steel toilet with an attached sink was off the front left hand side. There was one itchy wool blanket and a cold cement floor.

I could hear a drunken male, hollering profanities from a nearby cell. I felt uneasy and scared. The bars provided a sick sense of security. I sang in order to muffle out the terrible sounds.

The first night I woke abruptly from my sleep. Two officers were valiantly trying to calm me down.

"You're okay. You were having a nightmare. You were screaming and looked as if you were defending yourself. We tried talking to you from the bars, but you weren't responding. Do you remember what you were dreaming about?"

"No."

"Would you like a glass of juice?"

"No, thanks."

The following morning a pleasant young officer came to my cell.

"Hi Laura, I'm Constable Ben." he stated. "I understand you'll be spending the day with us. May I please have your blanket? Nobody here is allowed blankets during the day here. What can I grab you for breakfast, a donut, a cinnamon bun?"

"Whatever, it doesn't really matter. I'm not hungry anyways." I replied.

"There is going to be a court hearing for you some time this morning. You'd be better off with something in your stomach," he said.

"I'll have the cinnamon bun," I answered.

Ben came back with breakfast on a tray. He opened the cell door and placed it on top of the mattress. He hung around for a few minutes talking with me.
"Laura, I'm going home at lunch. My wife has lots of magazines. Can I bring you a couple? What kind do you like to read?"

"Anything but sports."

Shortly after breakfast, two different guards showed up at my cell, one female and one male.

"We're here to take you to your court hearing. You'll have to wear handcuffs, until we bring you back to your cell. That barrette in your hair needs to be removed, so that you don't hurt yourself with it. You're on suicide watch and we're not taking any chances. Your mother informed us that you're suicidal."

"God help me," I prayed in silence, as I walked cuffed between them down the long cold dingy hallway.

A prosecutor in the court room read an order for a psychiatric assessment from my previous psychiatrist. The judge granted the order. I was stuck between a rock and a hard place. I was to be flown back to Edmonton, escorted by two officers.

I was escorted out of the court room by the same guards.

"This isn't right or fair," I stated out loud. "If only they knew the truth."

Minutes after being locked back my holding cell, Ben was there.

"Laura, what would you like for lunch? I have some TV dinners. Which would you prefer the chicken or the beef?"

"Chicken would be nice."

Ben brought me lunch and sat with me while I ate.

"Is everything okay?" he asked.

"The lunch is good."

"You seem down, since returning from court," he mentioned.

"It doesn't matter, nobody ever listens," I replied holding back tears.

"If you need to talk to someone, I'm here," he offered.

"Thanks for the offer."

The following morning two new male officers were at my cell.

 "Laura, we're here to bring you to the airport. I'm going to handcuff you before you leave your cell. I have your purse with me. Do you like the way I'm carrying it?" the taller cop's joked.

I didn't appreciate his comments. I chose not to respond to him. I already felt degraded, by this mocking approach. I knew this day would eventually end, but the bitter memory would be mine to keep.

I walked in handcuffs between the two officers through the crowded Vancouver airport. Strangers at the airport noticed and stared with curiosity as we walked by them through the building. This event topped my list for one of my most embarrassing and humiliating experiences.

They took me down to the airport's prison cells and placed me in a holding cell. Two female cops from home eventually showed up at my cell.

"Laura, I'm Nancy and this is my partner Megan. We're bringing you back home for an assessment."

Again, I was handcuffed and ordered to walk between them. We approached the boarding area and the flight staff requested our tickets.

"Here are our tickets and one prisoner," Nancy declared.

"Laura, I'm taking off your handcuffs for the flight. When we get on the plane, you're to sit between us."

After the plane took off, breakfast was served. Nancy and Megan were decent and respectful to me.

"What do think of everything that's happening to you?" asked Megan.

"It's not right or fair," I answered.

"What would you like to see?" asked Nancy.

"I deserve a fair assessment, which won't happen if I fall into the slimy hands of my previous shrink. I should be brought to the mental hospital, seeing how I'm being labeled as mentally unstable, instead of him. Hopefully someone will see," I replied.

I was never handcuffed again. After we landed the ladies drove me out to the mental hospital.

Once I arrived at the facility, I was interviewed by two different psychiatrists. The second doctor spent more time discussing in depth, details of my life.

"Laura, I don't see any reason for you to be here. You're not crazy and you're not mentally ill. These visions you have are a gift. You've had a very rough life. I can see you're hurting, but you refuse to cry. If I call Social Services and placed you in a foster home tonight, would you promise to stay with them until your eighteenth birthday?"

"That would depend on how I was treated. If they treat me fine, I'd stay. If I'm mistreated, I'll leave."

"In seven weeks you'll be eighteen. Why don't you stay here? As soon as you're of age, we'll help you find an apartment of your own. I'll make it worth your while. Free run of the facility, swimming, and unescorted shopping trips to town, baking and different functions. What about waitressing in our coffee shop? This would be better for you than taking a chance on a foster home. Your mother will cause major problems for everyone, if you walked away from a placement."

I looked him in the eyes.

"Are you really promising to let me go on my eighteenth birthday?" I asked.

"Yes, you're free to go," he said. "I don't want to see anybody mistreat you. You've been through a lot."

Two weeks after arriving, there was a patient council meeting and election going on. I decided to join them. Within the hour I was both nominated and elected president of the patient's council. I attended a ribbon-cutting event during my stay. A building on the property was being named after an influential lady.

The following weekend, a staff member took me to her cottage for the weekend. I had a lovely time with June and her husband Larry. I enjoyed playing with their dog.

The following weekends, I went home with other people. I started enjoying myself with their families.

One evening my doctor was working late. I was talking to him when he offered to take me for dessert at the staff cafeteria. I was excited, he was preoccupied, and we forgot to tell the staff, where we were going. We drove in his beater to the other building.

"I'm surprised you don't drive a new car," I mentioned.

"I'm new to Canada. I've just brought my family over and money is tight," he responded.

We were finishing our dessert when an alarm was set off. At the same time his pager started to beep. He excused himself from the table and made a quick phone call.

He returned to the table a minute later.

"I should have told them we were going for dessert before we left," he said. "They were doing the final head count of the evening before locking the unit door. They assumed you took off. I just let them know that you're with me. Don't worry, you're not in trouble."

One afternoon I had a premonition of a female patient dying. I mentioned this to the staff right away. Twenty four hours later this lady died. I was returning from lunch when I spotted a gurney with a body in a body bag. I could see it being pushed down the hallway. A couple of staff members sat with me and we grieved the female patient's death together.
I was given an IQ test, achieving just two points below genius! The doctor said it was probable that, had my childhood been more stable, my test would have resulted in a much higher score.

The week before my eighteenth birthday, Nancy a nurse at the institution, grasped the dynamics of my situation when I received a call from my mother. Nancy realized that the call upset me and, as I retreated to my room in tears, she followed me inside.

"Laura, I'm really sorry about what happened to you. We've got the wrong person in here. What I heard on the phone tonight was sick, controlling, abusive, and completely uncalled for."

"I'm okay, it doesn't matter."

"We've been watching you for awhile. Every time you receive a phone call from her, your whole demeanor changes. You appear distressed and uneasy. Tonight I listened in on your phone call. I needed to know what was happening. This is going to be documented and a meeting will be held tomorrow. I'm putting in an immediate request for an apartment or accommodations of your choice."

A couple of choices were presented to me the following day.

The apartment they were offering wasn't the best choice. This apartment would be shared with a roommate. I would have to enroll in a program teaching young people how to survive on their own. I already knew how to cook, clean, shop, and work.

My biggest concern was my education. I was going to be an adult in a couple of days and I didn't even have a grade eight education.

Another choice was Inga, an older lady offering room and board. I felt her place would be in my best interests. It would only be she and I living in the household. I registered at a local high school as a mature student. It bothered me that I was older than the other students. I took correspondence courses and worked as a babysitter while attending high school.

Inga was spiritual herself. One evening she insisted that I attend a supper with a group of people she knew. Many of these people casually spoke with me. I knew they were observing me, but I didn't know why.
The next day when speaking to Inga, I could hardly believe what she was saying.

"Laura, you're special. Those people we had supper with last night are mystics. I asked them what they sensed about you. They say you have superior gifts and abilities. You need time to heal and release the negativity first, which has been inflicted your whole life. One day you will be somebody many will look up to and respect. You're going to help many people."

I stayed with Inga for a year. The following year, I rented an apartment with a friend. One night, I was out on the balcony enjoying the evening sky. I became aware of a looming tornado. I had never seen a tornado before. I went inside and told my roommate.

"Taylor, there's going to be a tornado!" I exclaimed.

"We don't have tornado's here. What makes you say that?"

"The sky is different and I sense it."

"I hope you're wrong," Taylor said.

"Me too."

Sixteen hours later a devastating tornado hit the Edmonton area, killing several people.

After being on my own for awhile, I started talking with mother. I forgave her and decided to work on our relationship. I desired the mother-daughter relationship I thought other girls had. Eventually she talked me into moving back home. We were going to catch up on missed time. I ended up regretting this decision.

Grade twelve was an interesting year for me. During the year, English became my favorite subject. One day, after school, I went to talk to my favorite English teacher about the details of an assignment.

"Laura," she said. "I can see you writing a book one day."

"I don't think so Mrs. Birch. Don't get me wrong. I like English, but I read and hand in assignments for marks. To write a book would be a huge undertaking, which I'm not prepared to do."

In Grade Twelve, I auditioned with my friends to become an extra in a documentary. We all made the audition. Outfits from the 1940's were issued to us on the first morning of the filming. We only had fifteen minutes to get dressed, before we were on.

The front of the blouse I was to wear wouldn't stay buttoned shut. Within seconds of complaining, the seamstress quickly sewed it shut while I was wearing it. The filming was interesting and exciting. I learned how movies were made.

The following day was to be the final day of the filming.

It was hard to fall asleep that night with all the excitement. While lying awake, I saw a vision of an empty stretcher beside me. I wondered why?

Over the past couple days my hips had become extremely tender. They snapped and crackled weirdly every time I moved. I assumed these were some sort of growing pains.

A friend's mother threw us a party after the filming was over. We spent the evening enjoying ourselves. I was sitting on the floor, when one of my friends asked me to dance. I sprang up to join him and my hip locked. I couldn't move from the waist down on one side. The pain was tremendous. My body went into shock.

An ambulance was called. I was taken to the hospital. A deformed muscle had dislocated ceasing the front of my hip joint, straining and tearing the other muscles and ligaments in my pelvis.

The condition worsened as time went on. The week before graduating, both hips froze. I was bedridden and missed my graduation.

Chapter Two

HEAVENLY BREAD

Nina invited me over to meet her father Sam, who was a psychic himself, visiting from Israel. He spoke limited English. We had heard about each other, but had never met. Nina was translating our conversation when the doorbell rang.

"Oh, I lost track of time. I promised to help Ruth with something. Hope you'll be okay without me for ten minutes," said Nina.

We both continued our visit despite the language barrier and discovered the energy of language. Communication vibrations are universal. I was able to understand Sam through energy, as he spoke Arabic, with the odd English words or short sentences thrown in. I could only respond in English. Sam was experiencing the same in reverse.

"Where in my house am I standing?" Sam demanded.

"I don't know. I can't do that." I hesitated unsure of my ability to see across the world. In the past I had unintentionally participated in remote viewing, but I'd never done so on command.

"Yes you can. Spirit tells me so." Sam insisted.

"You are in your yard at the side of your house. Your house is a sandstone color. There are two palm trees in the yard. I find the area extremely peaceful."

Sam's face lit up with great joy. "See, you did it."

"That's where I was. Thirty meters from my door is the cemetery."

We then decided to read each other. We exchanged palm readings, unaware Ruth was observing us from a distance.

"Excuse me, may I join in?" Ruth interrupted.

"Sure," we said in union.

"Can you look at my palm?" Ruth requested in desperation.

"Yes," said Sam.

"I'm worried about my health. Is my MS going to get worse?" Ruth handed her palm over to Sam.

"You have a few short years left. Something else will take you."

Ruth turned to me.

"Is my MS going to worsen?"

I closed my eyes. Ruth's physical appearance and health was the same as today. She never aged in the vision. This usually indicates death, but I didn't know why.

"Your MS is going to be like it is today."

Ruth thanked us and got up to leave. I felt uneasy as Ruth approached her car. Chills went through my body as she drove away.

Six weeks later, a strong presence could be felt lurking in the kitchen. Out of thin air several dimes struck the floor. Next a stack of papers came crashing down off a spotless countertop.

 Through causing a disturbance, a distressed soul was attempting to communicate.

This situation was interrupted by a phone call. "Laura, you remember my friend Ruth?" Nina asked in a distraught tone.

"Yes."

"Ruth and her husband Mike were killed in an accident last night. They were hit by a truck. There were no witnesses."

"I'm sorry to hear that. Are you okay?"

As Nina spoke, I could see the truck driver drinking several beers prior to driving. He had been travelling slightly over the speed limit. I chose not to say anything. This would have only upset her more.

"Laura, I can hardly handle this. Ruth and Mike were over visiting us last night. They never made it back home from our place. I can't believe they're gone. How are those poor children going to cope with losing both parents? Who's going to take care of them?"

As she talked, I closed my eyes and went to Spirit. The children were with an elderly couple.

"They will live with their grandparents," I said.

While consoling Nina, I felt a strong presence lurking in the kitchen. By evening, the earlier disturbances had ceased. Crawling into bed, I saw something odd. In the corner of the pink carpeted bedroom floor was a piece of bread.

I crawled out of bed to take a better look. The middle of the bread was missing. It looked as if someone had used a heart shaped cookie cutter.

While examining the evidence, I lifted the bread, and found the Roman number "II" was etched into the carpet, underneath the bread. In a moment of anxiety, I dropped the bread.

Above the bread a number "two" and the letter "X" were imprinted side by side. Six inches below the bread was a solid heart, drawn into the rug. Another six inches down was the Roman numeral IV slightly tilted to the right.

Immediately I understood the meaning. "Two X" represents the couple killed. A piece of bread represents the bread of life. The hollow heart over the "II" signifies their love for the two children. Solid heart represents the love they shared. Slanted numeral four reflects their fatality minutes before the fourth of the month.

I spent much of the evening in prayer and meditation.

"Spirit, please allow me to meet with the souls, who are leaving these messages. Watch over us, protect us," I begged.

While sleeping I slipped into astral travel. There was a heavy dense fog, making navigation awkward. Black iron gates and fencing could be seen in the distance. Beyond the gate was a dark ancient style building, with a purple dome. A breathtaking sunrise filled the morning sky.

Finally I arrived at an elegant gate. My main focus was to meet up with the restless souls. This environment was peaceful and inviting, I wanted more. While attempting to step through the gate, an invisible energy forced me backwards through a tunnel. I jumped with the impact of my arrival.

After this experience, I was unable to sleep. First thing in the morning, I called Nina.

"Hi, how are you doing?" I asked.

"Not so great. I'm going to Ruth and Mike's funeral this afternoon."

"Do you have a minute? I have something neat to tell you."

"Okay."

"I had some unusual spiritual disturbances linked to Ruth and Mike going on yesterday. Last night I had found a very descriptive message in my bedroom. This involved bread and drawings in the rug. Ruth and Mike used bread to symbolize the bread of life. Most of the message reflected love."

"Last night while sleeping, I astral travelled to the other side. I ended up at the gates of Heaven, for the first time in my life."

"Did you see them?"

"No, I was pulled away and sent back to my body, while attempting to step through the gate."

"Can you go back tonight and try to find them?"

"I shouldn't push the limits after being sent back. I don't know what the consequences would be."

"What if there was something else they needed to tell you?"

"They'll have to leave me a message."

"If anything else happens, let me know," said Nina.
"Okay," I responded.

Later on in the morning, I bumped into Constable Zach, who also knew Ruth.

"Hi, Constable Zach. Did the driver of the truck have enough alcohol in his system to successfully charge him with impaired driving?"

"Who have you been talking to? Who leaked you that information? That's classified police information."

"Nobody leaked anything to me."

"Laura, you have way too much information on this. Who were you talking to? The family doesn't even know about this."

"Constable Zach, I swear I didn't talk to anyone. I've been like this since childhood

Chapter Three
SPIRIT GUIDES

Mary Ellen

I first encountered Mary Ellen as a teenager. I did not know her name until much later. However, I was very aware of her presence just the same. It was she who saved me from falling into an open drain hole. I was out for a walk, not really paying attention to my surroundings when a loud decisive voice ordered me to 'Stop'. Two steps ahead, somebody had removed the grate off a drain hole.

For many years, I could only hear a female's voice belt out various verbal warnings.

"Watch out," a voice warned, saving me from being struck by a car.

Mary Ellen physically appeared to me years later. I had just woken up to discover a yellow beam floating in the room. The beam morphed into a beautiful dark haired, fair skinned lady of approximately forty. She wore a golden yellow gown with a matching bonnet. Her clothing style would be of the early 1900's. She looked smiling at me. "Hello," she said. I instantly recognized her voice.

"What is your name?" I asked.

"Mary Ellen," I understood through telepathy.

Dan

One evening, I was busy reading a client at the Capri Restaurant. A male spirit guide kept reappearing. After being interrupted three more times, I stopped the reading.

"Excuse me Sir, I need to stop your reading for a few minutes. An unfamiliar spirit guide is trying to communicate.

Please sit quietly. I need a couple of minutes."

Now the guide was hovering slightly above the table top in midair. He displayed himself from head to shoulders. A flame-like golden aura surrounded his white silhouetted body. This balding, blue-eyed male was roughly fifty years old. It took time to focus on his fair facial features. He spelled his name out one letter at a time mid-air D A N. After Dan's amazing introduction, he vanished for a couple days.

Dan regularly appears to me in full color or black and white. I've seen him wearing jeans, a shirt, a jacket and cap. Other times he wears a robe. I noticed him wearing glasses. Glasses are scholarly on the other side – nothing to do with vision problems.

Dan has been my main teacher over the past several years. I see and hear Dan. Awake, asleep or meditating. He spells letters, words and numbers out in midair. Telepathy is often used during our communication.

On occasion Dan has rung my door bell, early in the morning, when I'm partially awake and lazing about. I have jumped out of bed struggling with my housecoat, running down the cold hallway and getting to the front door, just to find no one there, not even a footprint in the fresh snow.

Climbing back into bed and shutting my eyes, I could see Dan's smiling face.

"Forget it Dan, I don't do mornings!"

Occasionally my phone will ring once waking me. The telephone caller ID displays several zeros or nothing. Closing my eyes, I can see Dan grinning.

Experiences with My Guides
The following stories contain a few encounters, which I've had with my Spirit Guides.

39

The Stadium
Astral travelling happens when the soul ventures out of its earthly body, while remaining connected by the silver cord of life. This can happen while asleep or awake. These journeys can be either spontaneous or planned.

While sleeping, I spontaneously astral travelled. I found myself on the other side, in an empty ancient open air stadium. My spirit guide Dan was walking down a field with me. The communication was telepathic, which is a strong connection of thoughts, felt intuitively.

Dan and I started heading off the field and up the stairs. I suddenly noticed nine stones, the size of billiard balls, flying in midair towards me. These were racked in the traditional triangular formation used to start a pool game. Out of fear, I fled back to the safety of my body. Seconds later, I awoke, hearing and feeling the stones hit my spine from the bottom to the top.

I went to see my chiropractor the next day. I explained to him what had happened. He was shocked to find my back perfectly aligned. Prior to that day my back was never straight.

Crystal Ball
While gazing into a crystal ball, I've seen a couple of interesting things. I've seen an eagle flying about the crystal ball. One time the grim reaper appeared.

One afternoon I was gazing into my crystal ball, desperately wanting to know how I could succeed as a psychic medium, when Dan appeared! He had glasses on and was sitting at a desk. I focused on him, watching intently as he picked up a long pen. He started writing sentences on pieces of paper. I tried to get a closer look, but I was unable to read what he was writing.

The Book
I awoke from a dream. Dan appeared to me in a vision. He was smiling while holding my book half open, as if he had

been reading. He seemed pleased with the contents. The book cover seemed plain and incomplete to me.

Dan showed a boardroom with 3 men dressed in business suits. They were intrigued with my book, which was in the middle of a table. Ten months earlier I had seen one of these men shaking my hand.

The X-Ray

I had stepped on something, which seemed to be embedded in my foot. Days earlier a Doctor had ordered X-rays. While on the X-ray table, I was shown "X" and "S," which meant there was a something wrong.

The following day I was reviewing the film with a physician.

"Dr Green, my heel has a shape on it, which is shaded differently." I pointed this area out to him. "Could this be glass in my foot?"

"Glass would look different. This is probably entry point scar tissue, which we're seeing. Let's wait a week and see if it gets better. I really don't know if anything is in there. I'd rather not dig into your foot without being sure."

After returning home, I decided to soak my tender foot. I shut my eyes, while relaxing. Through a vision, I was shown to get a tea bag and soak it in hot water. I was to put it on my foot.

I retrieved my prune soaked foot from the water and dried it off. I limped into the kitchen and boiled some water. After heating the water, I steeped a cup of tea. I returned to the living room with a soothing cup of tea and a hot compress. I sat down and gently placed the tea bag on my foot.

Suddenly my foot ached. I closed my eyes and watched numbers being presented, as a count down "4"," 3", "2" and "1". Upon removing the compress, two pieces of glass were sitting on top of the tea bag. One was the size of a peppercorn.

"Is there any more?" I asked Dan the reply was "0."

The Dentist
At the dentist I was having two teeth pulled. Spirit kept displaying the two teeth. One had a big black mark and the other was pure white. I assumed one tooth down and one more to go. Suddenly my dentist stopped working and pulled off his mask.

"I have good news for you. The shadows on the x-rays showed both teeth needed fixing. After repairing the first cavity, the other tooth is fine. Sometimes x-rays can be misleading"

Spirit Guides
Spirit Guides are highly evolved perfected souls from heaven. Our guides are not angels or loved ones. They know the lessons we need to experience to perfect our souls.

Everyone has at least one spirit guide. They can change at different points in our lives. Extra guides come and go when assistance is required. In certain situations guides and angels work together.

Relationships with Spirit Guides are individual. The soul has unique levels of development much like learning to talk. There is no pace, time frame or frequency during development. Communication with Spirit Guides can happen while meditating, waking or sleeping.

Guided meditation works well for beginners, freeing our minds and altering our energy. Meditation allows us an easier connection with Spirit.

Early Communication with Spirit Guides
Communicating with guides is different than our

conversations with each other. Spirit Guides may be awkward and hard to understand at first. Some people may wonder if they've lost touch with reality.

Early communication with guides can be very subtle and go unnoticed. An example: You're driving in an unfamiliar area without a map and you arrive at a set of lights. Deep inside something is telling you to turn right, even though you planned on turning left. After choosing to ignore the message you turn left and end up back tracking to the right.

Let's say someone is trying to nail down a time frame on finishing a project. "Yes, we should be able to complete this within seven weeks. Sorry, I meant seven days." The word "weeks" had been unintentionally blurted out. A conscious effort is made to correct the statement. Seven weeks later the project was complete. Most of us are unaware of this early subtle contact with guides.

The first message could be a meaningless letter of the alphabet or a number shown repeatedly. This is like flashcards shown randomly. These are used as a tool to see if you are paying attention. Later on, the flashcard scenario may be packed full of information. This becomes a way of downloading knowledge on future events. Another comparison would be the black numbers, which were used to count down the start of old films, on a white screen.

Once you establish a relationship with your spirit guide, there will be boundaries. Guides have their own protocol on how they choose to assist you. Calling upon your guide doesn't guarantee answers or an immediate visit. Sometimes a flood of information is received. Other times only part of the answer is supplied. There will be frustrating times, when no answers are revealed. Spirit gives us what we need, not necessarily what we want.

Communicating with Spirit
While guiding a group of beginners into meditation, at Mystics Metaphysical Shop, an unfamiliar Spirit Guide

joined us. She was standing in front of me. I felt distracted. "Excuse me, Spirit, Why are you here?" I silently asked.

"To help the others see," the guide whispered. I went on to lead and complete the meditation with her.

I saw some of the interactions that some group members experienced during their meditation. After the meditation, I was preparing to lead the group discussion. I knew most had something interesting happen. I allowed each student a brief moment to share their experience with the group. Out of the corner of my eye, I noticed movement. The pendulums on display were moving in a swinging motion. There was no air conditioner or fan in the area causing this movement.

"Could I ask everyone to look over at the pendulum display? Those pendulums are being manipulated by energy. There is a lot of spiritual activity in here, let's experience it." We quietly watched the swinging pendulums for awhile.

"The power of Spirit is amazing. Let's go around the circle and share what we experienced during meditation."

"Yvonne, I heard you let out a shriek during meditation. What happened?" I asked.

"Out of the blue, this guy was sitting there looking at me, resting his head on his hand. He was right in my face."

"Did he say anything?"

"No, I just wasn't expecting this. He seemed to be sitting there, waiting for an answer."

"Debra did you experience anything?"

"Yes, the face of an elderly lady with wrinkled yellowish skin appeared. It was hard to see her eyes with all the folds and creases."

"Your guide is a very old soul," I replied. "Did anything else happen?"

"Yes, I've always suffered from ADHD. This was the first time in my life that I have sat still. I have never been this relaxed, even while medicated."

"Possibly your ADHD may have been mistaken with spiritual restlessness."

"Jason, what was your experience?"

"My deceased brother was sitting by a lake. He invited me to stay awhile. We sat there watching the ripples in the water."

"You realize you're deceased brother isn't your spirit guide. During meditation we can meet up with loved ones. Sandy, do you have something to share?"

"A hand was presenting a bouquet of flowers to me. After a couple minutes, I could see the face of a smiling man wearing a fedora. He carried a pointer stick and drew the name Michael in the sand. I asked him if his name was Michael and he nodded yes."

"Angie, you seem disappointed. What happened?" "All I saw was color swirls and felt peaceful."

"Don't worry. Seeing color is part of this experience. The rest will eventually follow. Gary, would you care to share?"

"I floated around watching the others meet up with their guides. After a while, an eagle flew by me. I was shown a special feather, which will be given to me. I went on to participate in a spiritual ceremony."

"Maxine, tell us your experience?"

"I could see a ballerina dancing and twirling about, but nothing was ever said to me."

"Maggie, what happened to you?"

"When I shut my eyes everything went black. I took the time to relax."

"Your third eye is undeveloped. With practice and perseverance this will change."

Spirit versus Ultra Sound

When I'm working with clients their guides are always present and usually visible to me. There are times when I can't see their guides. Instead I am flooded with information, which is similar to a fast paced slideshow. I find this particular type of connection more helpful.

Sheena had come in for a reading. I connected with her guide immediately. Relevant information pertaining to Sheena's future was being disclosed.

"Laura I need to ask you something."

"Sheena, please wait a minute, allow me to start first."

Sheena's guide was smiling while displaying an embryo enclosed in a lit up uterus.

"What is the arrival date and gender of this baby?" I silently asked her Spirit Guide. I received a letter "S" and a number "7" drawn in mid air.

"Is September 7th the arrival date?"

Instant chills entered the crown of my head. Then continue to circulate throughout my body. This happens when I hit things bang on.

"What is the sex of the baby?" I silently asked her Spirit Guide. The display of her womb lit up in pink.

"A girl," I quietly questioned and I felt the chills again. "Congratulations Sheena, you're pregnant!"

I watched her jaw drop in total surprise and her eyes welled up with tears.

"Are you sure I'm pregnant? We've been trying for years."

"Your baby will be born on September 7th."

"Do you know what I'm having?"

"A girl," I replied.

Sheena's spirit guide was giggling happily.

"Sheena do you still have a question for me?"

"No, you already answered my question about a baby. Is she healthy?"

I went to Sheena's Spirit Guide who displayed the letter "F" for fine.

"She is fine."

A couple months later Sheena was on the phone highly upset and crying.

"I had an ultra sound this morning. The technician told me the baby's a boy. I've spent weeks working on a nursery for a girl. I went on a shopping spree and purchased many expensive outfits for her. Can an ultra sound be wrong? Could you be wrong?"

I closed my eyes and went to Spirit.

"Dan, please help us. What sex is this child?" Right away, pink was shown. "Are you sure Dan?"

A newborn baby was shown, bundled in a light pink blanket. A tiny hot pink ribbon was tied to her dark curly hair. "Thank you Dan."

"Sheena, I still see a girl."

"What about the ultrasound? What if you are wrong?"

"I've been shown a girl. I stand by my word."

Sheena was still extremely upset even after I reassured her. Four months later I received a call.
"Hi Laura, I had a baby girl last week on September 7th. We called her Amanda."

The Guilty One

Verbal communication does happen. Usually it is short commands such as "stop" or "look behind you." Guides have been known to lip-synch.

Sophie came to me with a difficult family situation. Several of the family members were accusing each other of stealing. Upon connecting, Sophie's guide was displaying a hand stuffing papers into a pocket. I was trying to grasp the details being relayed. I stopped in total frustration halfway into the reading. Sophie's Spirit Guide stood in front of me with a stern look on his face shaking his head.

"May I have your name?" I asked.

"Sid," he telepathically replied.

"Sid, I need your help. Can you tell me who's guilty?"

Sid had his head turned sideways and had lip-synched something.

"I can't understand this way! I couldn't see your lips. Can you repeat yourself?"

"Father," he whispered in a raspy voice. "Thank you, Sid."
"Sophie, your Spirit Guide Sid just told me "Father" in plain English. I heard him with my own ears."

Mother Stands

Tyler had come to see me for a reading.

"Laura, I keep seeing the face of a man. He randomly appears, when I'm relaxing with my eyes shut. I don't know him. Do you think I'm seeing a ghost?"

"No, ghosts don't appear that way. This male is your Spirit Guide."

"That's odd." "Why?"

"Last week, I found my elderly mother standing on top of her bed, looking contently at the ceiling. She's been confined to a wheel chair and unable to stand for many years. In a panic, I quickly helped her back into bed. My mother insisted a pretty lady wearing a long blue gown appeared to her. Did she experience a ghost, spirit guide or is this dementia?"

"Your mother's spirit guide appeared."

Departure Dreams

Elderly friends have called me after experiencing these dreams. While sleeping some people visit the other side, prior to death. The person is approached by their spirit guide in a beautiful setting, such as a park.

An invitation is extended, such as "I have the perfect place for you. Would you like to stay awhile?"

An elderly widow had a familiar man, whom she couldn't place, proposed to her.

"Mildred, will you marry me. I already have a beautiful dress for you to wear."

"Not right now," she replied.

To accept the invitation would likely mean passing while asleep. To decline the offer, one should realize the time is near. Some people are very firm about needing to get back to something right away. Others find themselves among people who have been gone a long time. They are mingling with them and enjoying themselves.

Spirit Guides Use Codes

Spirit does use codes such as "Y" for yes or "O" for no. Other common codes seem to be "X" for wrong or problem and "S" for is. When I'm correct "S", becomes visible in midair. This is similar to someone nodding their head in agreement, while listening to someone speaking. I can see these codes with my eyes open or shut, while conversing with others.

The Boyfriend
Wendy had come in for a reading.

"I'm having trouble with my boyfriend Justin. Is our relationship going to be okay?"

With open eyes I viewed a big "O" drawn in midair. I went on to ask her guide, "Is their relationship over?" Letter "Y" was with a lit up background, which meant yes.

"Wendy this relationship is shown to be over." "Has Justin been telling me the truth?"

I closed my eyes and "X" was displayed with a dark background. "No."

Chapter Four

TRIALS AND TRIBULATIONS

I met Derek when I was twenty four. After dating him for a few months, he asked me to move in with him. I immediately accepted his invitation and left Mother's home. I moved out of town into his lakefront partially built abode in the middle of nowhere.

I had self esteem issues stemming from my life events. After everything I'd been through, I was surprised a man would actually want me. I was glad that I was good enough for someone. He treated me better than Mother did.

It was the week before Derek and I would tie the knot. One afternoon, while scrubbing the floor, I heard Mary Ellen's voice warn:

"This is what it is. It won't be great: This marriage will last 10 years and then there will be someone special to spend the rest of your life with!"

After hearing the shocking revelation, spirit went on to display the rest.

I was shown a shorter smaller framed man approximately 50 years of age. He had a lovely smile, glistening eyes and a receding hairline. He was wearing a blue dress shirt and grey pants. I was shocked I would go for an older man again.

Derek was almost 20 years older than me and very controlling. He was a bad boy. Derek spent most of his time intoxicated or causing grief. The only commonality we shared was breathing and parenthood. My hopes were, if Derek was loved enough, he would come clean, stop misbehaving and become a family man.

The following morning was extremely busy and the phone rang. "Good morning, may I please speak to Laura?"

"You're speaking to her," I replied.

"My name is Judy Gregg and I'm a marriage commissioner. 1 understand you are getting married and I'm calling to offer my services. I got your name from a list."

"No thanks, we already have someone. Goodbye!"

I hastily hung up the phone. I wondered if marriage commissioners were short of work and soliciting people with marriage licenses. The phone rang again.

"Hi Laura, its Judy, please let me explain. Allan Blunt your marriage commissioner had a heart attack last night and didn't survive. I have been asked to call his clients and assist them. I am offering my services to you for your wedding this coming Saturday. Can we set up a meeting for tomorrow at your place? What time would be better three or four pm?"

"Three o'clock would be fine." I replied.

Judy and I met the following day and we started to discuss the wedding vows. I sat for a few minutes reading the different vows, which could be used for the ceremony.

"Laura do you want the traditional vows? Where you promise to love, honor, and obey?"

"No, that doesn't work for us." The words honor and obey were way too powerful for an already controlling man.

"What about the alternative vows. Do you prefer them?"

"Yes, those vows are suitable."

The following Saturday Derek started drinking in the morning. We had an argument at lunch time and married two hours later. Derek was consumed with getting drunk and high during the reception. He spent most of his time ignoring me on our special day. I felt empty and alone at our wedding. I ended up going for a walk with friends.

Derek and I were the last to leave our reception at four in the morning. He had to finish off the keg of beer. After arriving at the honeymoon suite, Derek passed out. He reeked of alcohol and weed. I watch bitterly as my intoxicated husband slept, instead of consummating our marriage.

Months after marrying Derek, I found a carnival employee identification card while sorting through his office.

Oh My God, I freaked. He's the creeper, who was bothering my girlfriends and me at the summer fair when I was 19. He was such a disgusting loser that we refused to go on the ride he operated. I remembered him because he was so freaky. Now I was married to him. If those girls only knew, I would never be able to live this down. Before I unknowingly met Derek again he'd cleaned himself up and dropped the hippie look.

Derek became more unreasonable and unpredictable as time went on. He became increasingly involved in criminal activity, which fed his addictions. One evening, Derek put his arms around me while I was doing the supper dishes.

"I'm going to get rid of Dale Cardinal."

"Why?"

"That stupid cocksucker is costing me too much money in the courts. This whole thing has become costly, because the bastard won't pay his bill. Dale and his wife are lying pieces of shit. His lawyer always re-examines everything. I worked hard on his job and should be paid more. The cry baby complains about the work being sloppy and not within code. The stupid dick thinks he's perfect."

I was sickened and concerned that he would kill this man.

Looking him in the eyes, I said, "Last week someone on the jobsite caught you smoking up during coffee. A couple of days ago you returned to the jobsite intoxicated after lunch. Perhaps now's the time to get some help and clean up your act, before it's too late."

"I'm going to take my gun out of the garage wall and shoot him."

"Derek if you shoot him, you'll go to jail."

"That bastard is going to splatter and hit the ground like this." Derek headed to the living room. He fell to his knees while laughing hysterically. His face was beet red. He continued to display how Dale was going to hit the ground after he shot him.

"Only we'll know who killed him."

"Derek you'll get caught and end up in jail for the rest of your life."

"It would be worth it."
"Why?"

"God you're stupid! I just told you why! Weren't you listening?" Derek freaked.

"You'd think he'd stop the court thing. Nobody likes him. Last week a bullet went through his kitchen window, lodging into a wall. A couple days later that bastard's house caught fire."
"Did you do those things to him?"

"No, but it was a great idea," he proudly stated with the

look of accomplishment on his face.

I quietly went to spirit and asked for verification on the alleged activities. I was shown not only those activities, but others. Spirit had shown me Derek being escorted by security out of a building dressed in a parka, toque, and sunglasses.

"Derek you were removed from a government office by security disguised in winter clothing. What is this? Christmas in July? Do you realize they could have charged you? I guess that would only add to your collection of records."

"Who told you?"

I ignored his question.

"I was trying to visit Dale and everybody got excited," he complained.

"One of the wives is going to walk before the court case is over," I blurted. That bastard deserves to lose everything including his wife."
"How can you be sure it will be Dale losing Gail?"

"That would serve him right. Grab me a glass of milk, my stomach's acting up."

I had gone to Spirit while grabbing his milk. I was shown a food buffet with five heaping plates of food with a dancer's stage nearby.

"Why didn't you control yourself at the lunch buffet today? You ate five platefuls of fatty foods down at Boner's strip joint. Lean meat and vegetables were available. I don't understand why you come home to me after being over there. You know how I feel."

"I was hungry and the food is good. Were you following me?"

"I don't need to, I was shown."

"Who told you?"

"Spirit."

"You stupid crazy bitch, I don't know how you come up with this shit! Spirit doesn't exist."

"You're a sick man." "I'm fine."

"You need to see a doctor. You have diabetes, heart and liver disease."

"Do not. You're out of your mind."

"You might have a chance to save your life, but you'd have to change."

"You're full of shit."

"Say Hi to Jesus for me, when you get to the other side," I replied.

His energy momentarily shifted; he actually heard what I said. It was as if his soul had awakened for a few seconds. Bastard actually had a soul. I had never seen him like this in the entirety of our relationship.

"Jesus! What the hell do you mean? Do you think I'll ever have a chance of making it to heaven?"

"Anything is possible, if you change your ways. Otherwise you'll be detained and restricted after passing, if Spirit doesn't choose to cut you from existence upon arrival." I replied.

"What do you know about this anyways? Who's been feeding you this shit?"

"Out of curiosity, I asked Spirit what happens to evil people, after they die. Right away, I was shown white rolled out dough. The dough was being cut with a cookie cutter, by the hand of Spirit. The cut-out was discarded leaving a void, where it had been. Spirit's white hands were moving in a rubbing motion together, like washing their hands of the situation."

"I was planning on going to hell after I died. You know, how I always say may it be as much fun in hell as getting there. I meant it. I'm not a Christian; I'm an atheist or agnostic."

"Derek, atheists don't attend church. Why do you insist on going to mass every Christmas?"

"I always did as a boy, it isn't Christmas without mass."

"Why would you care about celebrating? You just told me you don't believe."

"It's just the way I was brought up. I enjoy celebrating holidays."

That night in the bedroom Derek placed a crisp $50 bill on my pillow.

"What can I get for this?" he inquired.

"Not much," I said grabbing the fifty and placing it in my night stand drawer.

Derek was horrible in bed and no amount of money could improve this.

A couple of days later I accompanied him to the doctor's office for an appointment and a week later for his test results. As the doctor read his test results, everything was revealed. His diabetes, cholesterol and liver diseases were out of control. He was angry, and informed the doctor the tests were wrong and demanded to be retested. Upon receiving his second batch of test results Derek came home fuming.

"You should have been a fucking doctor."

Derek grabbed a bag of cookies and a huge glass of milk and headed for the living room.

"You shouldn't be eating the cookies."

"Shut up."

The next day after testing his blood for sugar levels Derek became angry. He leaped from his chair and chased me around the main floor with a dirty used lancet. I ran and managed to safely lock myself in the bathroom.

"You fucking bitch! Do you know how this feels? It's your fault."

"Spirit protect me," I quietly begged.

About ten minutes later I heard Derek leave the house. Minutes later I could hear his truck drive away. I was safe.

I felt the need to get away. I had been missing my friend Agatha. A couple of days at the east coast with her would be perfect. I called Agatha and made arrangements to stay with her.

I let a few days pass before mentioning this to Derek. He refused to let me go, unless I brought him along. I called Agatha informing her Derek would be tagging along.

"Does he have to come with you?" Agatha asked.

"He won't let me leave without him."
"It won't be the same with him here. My children will be home and it would be nice for the two of us and the kids to visit without your husband. Can we get together another time without him?"

"I really need a break Agatha. I've arrange for my children to attend children's camp. I won't be bringing them."

"What's wrong?"

"Can we still stay with you?"

"Yes," Agatha said, with hesitation in her voice.

After hanging up the phone, Derek asked if everything was a go.

"Yes."

"Laura, we could head to a nude beach for a day."

"No Derek, you could head off to a nude beach on your own. Maybe you could find a good catch. Having me around would dampen your chances."

I could hear Mary Ellen, whispering "safety in numbers." That was odd. Safety in numbers had been my train of thought lately.

"Derek, you know you can't bring drugs on the plane, right?"

"Why would I bring a sandwich to a buffet?"

We boarded our flight to Agatha's days later. Derek and I chose to sit a couple of rows apart. The airplane had just taken off. I could feel tension and panic setting in. My heart started to race and it was hard to breathe.

"Are you okay?" a stewardess inquired.
"I'm okay. I'm fine, just a little stressed," I replied.
This wasn't normal for me. I closed my eyes and asked Spirit if I was having a heart attack. Within seconds I was shown an image of Derek smuggling drugs on board with him. His illicit drugs were concealed in a Tylenol tube in his pocket. His joints were hidden in his wallet between

twenty-dollar bills. My heart suddenly started pounding harder. If that filthy bugger got caught, I knew I'd be in trouble too. The only reason I was still with him is I feared for the safety of our children. Had I been single I would have been long gone. I started pondering the idea of him finding another interest and moving on. I'd gladly set him free.

I was glad to arrive at our destination. I took Agatha aside and briefly informed her of the situation.

"Too bad you didn't leave him at home," Agatha spoke trying to conceal her agitation.

"He wouldn't allow me to come without him," I answered, hoping she understood my predicament.

"That bastard better behave, my husband won't put up with this."

"Agatha I'm sorry, I needed a break and I feel safer around others."

"I'm going to warn Joseph before anything goes wrong. Hopefully he won't ask you to leave."

The next morning upon awaking, Derek was gone. He showed up for breakfast a couple hours later intoxicated.

"Where did you go, Derek?" I asked.

"I woke up at five am and couldn't sleep. I went out for a walk. I came across this guy setting up his garage sale and helped him."

I knew he was lying. He was out getting high. While exploring the new area, he lost track of time and direction.

"We're heading to town today; perhaps you should stay here and relax."

"Are you headed to the nude beach?"

"No Derek, we are heading to town."

"What about the nude beach?"

"Why don't you find out where it is and we'll drop you off on our way to town."

"Alone."

"Yes, by yourself."

Derek ended up coming to town with us, after he promised to stop talking about nude beaches. Agatha didn't want her children exposed to that sort of talk.

Later in the afternoon Derek noticed a marina at the edge of town. He wanted to stop and inquire about rentals. Derek came out of the shop beaming.

"I rented a boat for us to enjoy. It's my treat."

Suddenly, I remembered a vision of three girls crying on a deck this morning. I felt panicky, something wasn't right. Something bad was going to happen, but I didn't know what. I was reluctant, but we headed out on the water.

"Agatha, I'm scared!" I quietly told her.

"Don't worry. Safety in numbers. We'll be just fine."

After leaving the dock, Derek cracked open a can of beer and started drinking. He was stoned prior to departing. The ocean water was choppy. He started driving the speed boat erratically at excessive speeds and heading further out. The front of the boat was starting to go down a bit. There was approximately three inches of water on the boat floor. The waves of the ocean were coming in and hitting us. Many times the water forcefully struck our faces making it hard to breathe. I can recall choking on the salty ocean water, which also burned my eyes. "Derek, turn this boat around and head back now."

"Shut up, you stupid bitch. You always ruin my fun."
I quietly retreated to the back of the boat and took a seat. I wondered if I could somehow grab Joseph's cell phone if it would work. Would 911 bring us a coast guard? What could I hit Derek with to take him down? There was plenty rope to tie him. I quietly called on Spirit for assistance.

"Derek," Joseph shouted, "all of us are going to die out here if you don't turn this boat around. Four people died out here last week the same way. We're headed for disaster. My children are crying. Please let me drive the boat back."

"Joseph, are you a man or a pussy?" hollered Derek.

Derek was making light of the whole situation, mimicking and gesturing every move or sound Joseph made. Joseph started to cry. Derek was too intoxicated to realize the danger we were in. Agatha had never seen me retreat before and knew something had to happen quickly.

Agatha calmly approached Derek. "Look at my children, they're terrified. Would you do this, if you had children of your own? Do you want them to fear boating? Let's slow down the boat and turn it around. We'll stop at the closest dock and let the children out."

Derek immediately slowed the boat down and turned it around. Ten minutes later he pulled up to a dock of a shipping yard. A sign read 'No Trespassing'.

"Do you want to drop the kids off out here? This is a long way from town," Derek said to Agatha.

"They'll be fine. I'm going to be with them," Agatha said "Pass me the rope. I'll hold onto the boat while Joseph assists the children."

Agatha's kids were safely on the dock with her. I was already making my way to the front of the boat.

"Laura, are you coming with us?" asked Agatha

"Yes."
"You're getting off the boat and leaving me alone?" Derek stated in a shocked voice.
"Yes, I am."

"You're no fun," Derek snapped in anger.

"This was supposed to be a treat. Do I need to bring the boat back alone?"

"I'll come with you, but we must operate the boat safely on the way back. Then we'll drive the car here to pick up our ladies," offered Joseph.

Agatha and I sat together having a tea before bedtime. We were catching up on the interesting details in each other's lives.

"Laura, I don't know how to tell you this. My daughter came to me earlier this evening, insisting that Derek came out here to kill you. Whatever you do, please be careful."

"I've been watching my back for a while now. Derek is mean and unpredictable, but I'm generally in the know before things happen."

After having tea, we headed to bed. Agatha's household was awoken by hysterical screaming.

"Get out. Get your naked body off my bed. Get your ugly body out of here," shrieked a child's voice.

"Shhhh! Shut up, I'm leaving," uttered Derek.

Agatha and I almost collided in the dark hallway running to assist the screaming child. Turning the corner, Derek was standing buck naked in the doorway of her youngest daughter's bedroom. Agatha shoved past Derek to console her daughter. I grabbed Derek by the arm and led him further down the hallway.

"What the hell are you doing? Why are you naked? What on earth were you doing in her bedroom? Did you touch her? What is wrong with you?"

"It seemed like a nice place to go."

"Pardon me?"
"You were snoring and I didn't want to disturb you. The bed was empty so I went to sleep."

Derek headed back to our room. I needed to see Agatha and her daughter.

I knocked on the closed bedroom door.

"Agatha, can I come in?"

"Yes."

I apologized to Agatha's daughter Stella.

While everybody was sleeping Stella had secretly stayed up to watch TV. She headed back to her bedroom to find Derek lying naked on top of her bed. He never touched her.

I helped Agatha change the bedding and they headed back to bed. I went back to our room. Derek had passed out. I sat in a chair across from the bed awake the rest of the night.
"What am I doing with this crazy bastard anyways," I silently questioned myself. I still had difficulty with the situation. Is this what Mary Ellen was referring to? Weeks prior, I was preparing supper at home. When I heard Mary Ellen's voice state "He's going to deviate sexually."

Derek was more than happy to arrive home the next day.

He was free to be intoxicated around the clock in his own domain. My friend Kate joined us for supper that evening. I was sickened by Derek's drunken behavior. I grabbed Derek's beer off the table and poured it down the kitchen sink. He left the table enraged and headed outside.

Minutes later he showed up at the kitchen door. He had a sledge hammer in his hands. His hands were clenched about six inches from the head of the hammer.

"You fucking bitch. You should learn to control yourself. That was my last can of beer. How dare you?"

"You had enough."

He started aggressively swinging the sledgehammer around. I kept a calm appearance. Seconds later, he took off to the yard with the sledgehammer. He was swinging it around randomly destroying items.

"Are you going to call the police Laura?" asked Kate.

"No Kate, it would take the police at least 25 minutes if not longer to get out here. If he was to catch me on the phone, things would get ugly fast. Safety is in numbers. I'm sorry you had to experience this. Please don't tell anybody. I'm not ready to leave yet."

"Let's take your car and leave."

"No Kate, we would have to drive past him, which would jeopardize our safety. Derek wouldn't hesitate to throw that sledgehammer through the windshield. Let's go for a walk. If we could go out the patio door and walk along the beach, he won't see us. He'll eventually calm down."

Kate hesitated, and then agreed to go for a walk. "Why don't you leave him?" Kate asked.

"I left him five years ago for a short period of time. One night

Derek invited Bruce and Liz over for supper. The men partied and became intoxicated. Later in the evening, Liz and I were walking beside each other towards the fire pit, when Bruce obnoxiously walked up to me and grabbed me by the breasts. I was humiliated, shocked and angry. Liz was livid with his actions and told this six foot six drunken idiot to apologize to me. He denied grabbing me and refused to apologize. I told Derek immediately and I requested that he ask his friend to leave. Derek thought it was funny and that I was over reacting and the partied on.

The following weekend Derek invited Bruce to stay the weekend. Derek and I had been arguing prior to Bruce and Liz arriving. Upon their arrival I could see grey shading all over Bruce's aura. Something was seriously wrong with Bruce. I quietly left the room, closed my eyes, and went to Spirit.

"What's wrong with Bruce?" I asked.
Right away I was shown Bruce's veins through out his body the letters H C were attached to his blood.

"Is this Hepatitis C?" I asked.

"Everything lit up. Spirit went on to show an urn surrounded by yellow grass. Bruce would be dying when the grass is yellow.

I went back to the kitchen. I started serving everyone a coffee and Derek excused himself to make a quick phone call. I decided to warn Bruce about where he stood with me, while Derek was preoccupied.

"Bruce I need to make something clear. I don't trust you after what you did to me last weekend. I don't want you here around me or my children. If you ever touch me again, I'll have you charged.?"

"Bruce, did you hear Laura?" piped up his wife Liz. "She means it."

"Yes," he sheepishly replied.

A couple of months later, a weak, decrepit apparition of Bruce appeared in our bedroom, shortly after going to bed. Bruce had a serious look on his face.

"Go away, get out of here" I ordered. I didn't want him anywhere near me, dead or alive. I reminded myself that there was a barrier between us, that he couldn't do anything to me. He looked at me as if he was begging for forgiveness.

"I forgive you, Bruce. Move along, you're not welcome here."

Bruce vanished into thin air. The next morning Liz called informing us of Bruce's death last night.

That same evening, Derek was out partying again. I became sick and tired of the whole situation and decided to leave with the children. I packed up our belongings and left.

The phone rang the following evening. "Laura I promise to stop drinking, if you come back." He started.

"What about the drugs Derek?"

"They're no big deal."

"Seeing how they're no big deal, are you willing to give them up?"

"I guess, obviously you don't want me to enjoy myself." "Not through intoxication, we don't deserve the misery it causes," I said.. "Are you willing to go for marriage counseling with me?"

"I will give up my bad habits and go to marriage counseling, but not until you return home. If you don't come home, I get every second week with the children by *myself.*"

This is terrified me enough to come home.

We had one appointment with a marriage counselor. Derek regressed back into his old habits a week later.

"Do you love him?" Kate asked.

"No, I fear him. He's very unpredictable. I have some control here. I fear for our children's safety. They'd be forced by law to have unsupervised visits with him. It would be dangerous to leave him. I'm scared of the consequences. You know the saying keep your friends close and your enemies even closer," I replied hoping she'd understand.

"Has he ever hurt you?"

"Not lately. Years ago he kicked me in the stomach so hard I couldn't breathe. My ribs and stomach hurt for several days. I threatened to leave him at that point and I should have. He promised to never hurt me again. If he becomes physical, it is more shoving, twisting wrists, a random punch, stepping on my toes purposely pinning my foot to the floor. Derek is generally emotionally abusive. On occasion, he becomes unpredictable and loses it, like tonight."

"I'd leave him, if I were you," Kate told me before she left for home. The moment Kate left, Derek came back inside.

"Bet you won't poor my beer down the sink again."
"Were you ever angry. What upset you about the situation?"

I asked trying to understand what was going on with him.

"I had a flashback of my drunken father losing it with me when I was sixteen. I poured his beer down the drain."

"Did he get out his sledgehammer too?" I inquired.

"Of course not, what are you, stupid? He didn't have one," he barked.

"That selfish fucker drank himself to death. The doctor warned him months before he died."

"So you're going to follow in his footsteps, and drink yourself to death?"

"No, I'm not as bad as he was. My health is better."

"Not with your recent bill of health. If you ever had a heart attack and stopped breathing, what would you want me to do?"

"Whatever you want at the time, it would be your choice."

"Would you want to be resuscitated or shall I let you go?"

"Your choice, whatever you want."

I decided that I didn't want to be saddled with expenses should he keel over. If Derek stopped breathing, I didn't want him back. The following morning, I made his funeral arrangements. I bought the wayward bastard a cheap pine coffin and a grave.

Before the meeting ended with the sales person, she asked if everything at home was fine. I told her everything was okay, but I knew deep down she realized something was wrong. I worried about her telling on me.

Hours later, the police were at our door. I panicked wondering, if I was in trouble for purchasing a casket and a plot earlier that day.

"Hello we're conducting a door to door search in this area for Randy Jones. Can I have your name, Sir?"

"Derek."

Laura Laforce

"Do you know Randy or have you seen him?" The officer inquired as he held up a photo of the missing man.
"No."

"Have you heard anyone speaking of him?"

"No."

"What do you think happened to him?"

"Oh he's probably had it with his family and has taken off to Vegas to start a new life."

"What would make you say that?"

"He hasn't been seen in weeks," slurred Derek through his drunken words.

"We need to ask your wife a couple of questions," mentioned the cop.

"What do you think happened to Randy?"

"He's dead," I started.

"Yeah, right Laura," interrupted Derrick.

"Let her finish," the eager cop demanded.

"There is a dangerous middle aged man living nearby, who killed him."

"Why would you say that?"

"I've seen the situation."

"Did you witness the murder?"

"No, I saw this through a premonition."

"Did you know the missing man?"

"No, never met him, but his soul is restless."

"Have you ever seen this truck?" the officer asked as he held up the photo.

"Yes."

"When did you see the truck?"

"Last week. The truck passed me on a back road and a blonde haired scruffy man was driving. I waved and he nervously waved back."

"Where was the truck headed?"

"The white truck was headed toward the city."

"Do you know the driver?"

"No," the driver seemed familiar and resembled the man I had seen in a vision. I wasn't prepared into further details with Derek present.

"Thank you for answering our questions. I need to visit other neighbors," the officer opened the door and left.

Several weeks later the man I saw driving the truck was arrested. Randy's remains were found on Leo's property. Leo was an acquaintance of Derek's. We had been introduced once several years back. Leo was later convicted of first degree murder.

Chapter Five

A MULTITUDE OF WARNINGS

Several years ago, Derek introduced me to his friend Veronica, a petite young looking Hispanic lady. Many envied her beauty; she easily trimmed fifteen years off her age. I always admired the recognition and success she held in the business community. A couple of times a year, she sat on the board of directors for the Women's Shelter.

I decided to stop by Veronica's house for coffee on the way home from shopping. While visiting, I started to feel uneasy. Veronica's energy was distorted and had drastically shifted from positive to negative. I could see darkness in her aura.

"Laura, I've been stressed lately!" said Veronica.

"What's up?"

"Things have been crazy. Last week I found a bug on my office phone. I brought it down to the police station. The cops questioned me for an hour. The government's been after me, they froze all my bank accounts. I've had people following me in vehicles."

"Who did you upset?"

"Remember my best friend Trudy?" Veronica asked.

"Yes."

"Well she and Lyle split."

"That's too bad."

"When they split, I started keeping Lyle company. Lately, I've been managing his excavating firm. After spending a couple of nights in bed with him, I got him to sell me his company for a dollar. Trudy won't be able to get her hands on anything," she laughed.

"Veronica what are you doing? Isn't Trudy your best friend?"

"She was my best friend."

"Why are you doing this?"

"Lyle's broken hearted."

"Can't you level with me?"

"You know Lyle's pretty lost right now, and he torments Trudy. Last week he almost chased her off the road," she laughed.

"Veronica, none of this is funny."

"Lyle's manic depressive and acts out. He even pisses off his employees. If he gets worse, I'll fire him. At least, I'll have his company including the fleet of vehicles," she confided.

I politely excused myself from coffee and left. "I'm going to have to watch my back with Veronica." I could only image what she'd do to me, if I left Derek.

A week later I heard Veronica had fired Lyle and took over his company.

A couple of days later, I received two visions warning of a car accident by a bridge. My small orange car was hit by a larger red car.

Months earlier, Spirit displayed a sequence of three brand-new cars. First was a yellow sporty car, then an orange car, followed by a short rear panel of a navy blue car. I drove a beater when this was shown.

"Why on earth would I have three cars?" I wondered.

I called the dealership and spoke with my sales rep, Dina.

"Hi Dina, this is Laura Laforce. Do you remember me?" I asked.

"Yes," she replied.

"I'm thinking about trading in my new car," I told her.

"Why?" she asked.

"I had a premonition about being in an accident with this car. I don't feel safe driving it." I responded hoping she'd put me into a different vehicle.

"You don't need to buy another vehicle. My friend's a psychic and she always able to avoid accidents," she calmly responded.

"No Dina, I don't have that much control. When I see something, it happens." I stated.

"Remember my brand-new yellow car, which was totaled by a semi at Christmas?"

"I'm surprised you lived."

"Me too. The head and neck injuries permanently cured my migraines. The vision only revealed the aftermath of the accident. I still don't remember the moving truck hitting us. This time I'm seeing the actual event. The idea of another one terrifies me. If I was to get hurt again, I might never recover."

"Give me a while. I'll get back to you."

The following morning I had a chiropractor's appointment to help loosen my injuries.

"How are you feeling?" Dr. Jones asked.

"Still very tender," I replied.

We chatted while he worked on my neck and back.

"What's new?" he asked.

"I recently received a vision of another accident involving a mid sized red car near a bridge," I responded.

"What are you going to do to avoid that?" he asked.

"I plan on avoiding major bridges and red vehicles," I replied.

Shortly after leaving his office on my way home, I noticed a red car, driving erratically, following me. I changed lanes only to have it do the same. Suddenly, it rammed into me. As the driver raced away, she looked right at me with a scowl. I managed to get the license plate numbers, before she raced out of sight.

The nerves in my arms were hurting making it almost impossible to hold my cell phone to either of my ears. My tailbone and my knee were aching.

A witness stopped to help me. He told me help was on the way. I asked him to call my friend Melanie, who worked a few blocks away. I found out later that Melanie couldn't leave work, so she called Derek, who also worked nearby.
Derek arrived at the scene of the accident. I watched him walking aggressively toward my car, failing his arms. Black negativity surrounded his aura. I was terrified. Derek arrived at the side window.

"Get out of the car, you stupid bitch," he ordered.

"God help me. Please don't let him hurt me," I silently prayed.

An ambulance arrived in the nick of time!

"I'm going to talk to them first and tell them how crazy you are," he threatened.

He raced off to meet them before they arrived at the vehicle. I could only imagine what he was up to. EMS started providing assistance. The paramedic attending said,

"We'll take you to the hospital and get these injuries assessed. Then you can talk to somebody special. I heard you were hit by a semi six months ago. Your husband says you have been different since."

I was in a lot of pain, but needed to release myself from this situation. This paramedic had bought whatever Derek told him.

"Do you think I'll be okay without medical assistance?"

"You'll definitely be sore for a while."

"I'm going to decline treatment. Let me go."

"She shouldn't go. She is really hurt," interrupted his partner.

"I'm fine. Let me be," I insisted.

After convincing them to release me, I was ushered to a police cruiser to fill out a report.

"Laura I've got bad news for you. The vehicle which hit you was stolen. We have already found the abandoned vehicle. Can you describe the person driving the vehicle?"

I went on to describe the driver as a female of native descent, with long brown hair. Then Derek tapped on the window of the police cruiser.

"The medics said she should have something to drink." He

passed a bottle of water to the officer.

The officer handed me the bottle of water. He sat observing my inability to open it.

"Here let me help you with that." He opened the bottle of water and handed it back.

"Take some sips before we carry on."

It took great effort to bring the bottle to my mouth, neither arm was working properly. After a few tries I managed to get a couple of sips. Tears welled in my eyes.

"Laura, you're hurt. After we finish, your husband should take you to the hospital."

He placed the clipboard with the report on my lap.

"I need you to fill out this part of the report for me." I attempted to pick up the pen only to end up in tears.

"Let me ask your husband to fill in the report. We're not allowed to write your report." The officer unrolled his window and called Derek over.

"I need you to fill out your wife's report, she is unable to write."
Derek obliged the officer and completed the report.

"Thank you for your help, Sir," said the officer.

"Your wife is hurt. Please take her to the hospital right away, to have her injuries treated."

"She's fine, she's just upset."

In anger, Derek erratically drove his truck from the scene. The officer briefly pursued his truck with flashing lights and warned Derek with a gesture, then drove off.

Upon arriving home, I opted to stay in our bedroom the remainder of the evening. The next morning it was difficult to move. My knee had popped out of joint. My hands and arms were extremely sore. I gradually made it down the stairs. I decided to pretend I was fine, it didn't matter how bad the pain was. When he was out of sight, I would eat enough to survive.

"Good morning," said Derek.

"Good morning," I replied.

"Are you going to make Sunday brunch?"

"No, I'm not hungry. Go ahead without me"

"Do you want a coffee?"

"No thanks."

The pain kept escalating. I could hardly function. I wasn't going to allow him to see this, if at all possible. It was a challenge to drink or eat with both my arms being hurt. I could hardly wait for Monday morning for Derek to go to work.

On Monday morning, Derek had noticed something wasn't right.

"You are hurt, aren't you?"

"No I'm perfectly fine, just the way you like me."
Derek was angry if anyone around him was ever sick or hurt. Unless he could see blood or vomit he would claim the person was faking it or mental. I patiently waited in agony for Derek to leave for work. I decided to get medical attention, but not until he was gone. I picked up the phone shortly after he left. I called the local health link wanting to know which emergency room had the shortest wait time.

"What's wrong?" asked the nurse on the phone.

"I was hurt on Saturday in a hit and run, and I'm finding it hard to sit, move or use my arms. I just need to be able to get in somewhere quickly."

"An ambulance should be sent to assist you."

"No, please don't send anyone. I live in a hamlet and other people would see and my husband would find out. I will find a ride in on my own."

"You're hurt though."

"Yes, but I'll get into trouble. Please just help me find a low waiting time."

"Do I understand correctly that you're not allowed to be hurt or sick?"

"Yes," I said hesitantly.

"That's wrong. How dare he treat you that way?"

"As soon as I recover, I'm leaving. Until then I need to stay."

The nurse provided me with the information I needed. I found a ride into town and received the medical help I needed.

Upon arriving home, I called on Mary Ellen.

"Mary Ellen you're right, this marriage isn't great; it's horrible. You're wrong about this marriage lasting ten years. Our eleventh wedding anniversary is coming up soon."

I sat waiting for some sort of reply and never received one.
A week later, my friend Shelly came over and joined Derek and me at the flaming fire pit.

"Laura, I can't wait for your fiftieth birthday!" said Shelley.

"Laura will be forty on her next birthday, not fifty," Derek attempted to correct her.

"Laura's planning on going to Vegas for her fiftieth birthday," stated Shelley.

"Why would you want to go to Vegas of all places? You're going to take me with you. Right?" he questioned.

"No Derek."

"Why?"

"You'll no longer exist in this life," I responded.

"What do you mean I no longer exist? I can go anywhere, I damn well please. I can sneak into the States."

"Derek you're going to die well before then," I casually replied.

"Us girls are going to Vegas, right?" inquired Shelley."

"No we're not going. My life will be very different then," I responded. This flowed out of my mouth, shocking me. I had not consciously changed my mind about travelling to Vegas. My life being very different had never occurred to me. That evening, Derek sat sulking on a bar stool in the middle of the garage, claiming nobody loved him. I felt great anxiety, knowing his gun was nearby.

The next morning I discovered a drawing on the television screen. Stick figures were etched into the dust. It seemed to have an airbrush appearance. There was no possible way for human fingers to achieve this. The messages drawn on the screen were similar to hieroglyphics. I identified my stick figure by the hair. I could see myself with circles around my head almost drowning. The two arrows which pointed east were very short. In the middle were three figures with four arrows pointing down. West on the screen were many arrows. A heart and a flower were displayed at the upper northwest corner of the screen. The heart represents love and the flower is growth. I realized by looking at the screen that my life was in danger. This was a display of a murder suicide.

My whole body started to shake with anxiety. I knew my life was at risk. It was time to leave. I had no money. My mobility was limited from the hit and run. I took a while to settle down. I couldn't let Derek see me this way. Somehow, I managed to regain my composure.

An hour later, Derek finally left for work. I waited another hour before calling the Women's Shelter. I informed the woman on the phone of my situation.

"Unfortunately, we're full. Can we send you to our next jurisdiction?"

"Yes."

After receiving the information I made the call.

"Unfortunately we have no space available until tomorrow at five pm. Can you find a way to stay safe until then?"

"Yes, this has been going on for years. I can manage as long as he doesn't catch us on the way out."

I gradually put some clothes and personal items together. Everything was slow going due to my injuries. I found my important papers, which also contained copies his criminal records. Then I grabbed my photo albums containing many memories. Derek had failed to come home that evening. About 11 pm the phone rang.

"Hi, Laura. I don't have enough gas to make it home. I'm going to sleep in the truck tonight."

"What time will you be home tomorrow?" "I should be home around supper time."
The next day I made sure the children were out on a play date. I didn't want them there if I got caught leaving. That way I could pick them up on the way to the woman's shelter. Derek arrived home at 2:30 in the afternoon. I was in the midst of removing the last plastic bag containing personal items. The plastic bag was on the verge of breaking. My heart raced. I calmly walked by him with the bag and sat it by the door.

"What are you doing?"

"Getting rid of some things I no longer need. I'm going to donate them to charity."

"Where's my coffee?"

"Give me a minute."

I put on the coffee and brought the last bag out to the car. I waited for the coffee to finish dripping and poured Derek a cup of coffee.

"Aren't you having coffee with me?"

"I'll grab mine in a minute."

I grabbed my coffee and joined Derek at the kitchen table.

"What do you have planned for supper?"

"We're having soup and sandwiches," I said.

"I have a couple of errands to run before supper.

"Kiss me before you leave," Derek demanded.

'You'll never have to kiss him again', I told myself. 'Pretend he's a filthy teddy bear. Kiss him and get out of here.' I gave him a quick peck on the lips and left the house.

Chapter Six

THE JOURNEY TO SAFETY

While heading towards the car, I called my dog. He came running towards me. I opened the car door and coaxed him in for a ride. I backed out the driveway for the very last time in my orange car. I dropped our dog off to stay at a friend's, until we were settled. Then I picked up the children from their friends place and we headed into town.

We arrived at the women's shelter in time for supper. During intake various reports were made. I was instructed by shelter staff to obtain an emergency protection order at the courthouse after the weekend.

"Do I legally need to tell Derek that I've left him?" I asked.

"Do you miss him?"

"No, I never want to see him again."

"Sometimes the ladies miss their husbands or boyfriends. When you're in the shelter you don't have to say good bye."

I was relieved I didn't have to let him know.

On Monday evening, I called Shelley from the shelter.

"Laura, what's going on? The police are looking for you. They've been calling me. Derek filed a missing person's report. Are you okay?"

"I'm safe."

"The police want you to call them. They want to talk to you. They say you're not in trouble."

"If you hear from them again, tell them I'm safe. I have to go now – somebody needs to use the phone. Goodbye."

Right away I notified the shelter staff. "The   police   are looking for me."

I was quickly ushered into the office. A staff member sat with me to assist me with the call. "Remember, we don't share the address with anyone, including the police. They can be provided with this phone number only."

My hands shook as I dialed the number for the police station. A lady's voice immediately answered my call.

"Police department. How may I direct your call?" she said.

"I was told to call the police. I understand they are looking for me." I said.

"Can I have your name?" she asked. "Laura LaForce" I responded.

"Hold for a minute." she ordered without waiting for my reply.

"Hello Laura" she said, "I'm putting you through to the sergeant. He wants to speak with you."

Immediately, the dispatcher put my call through to the sergeant.

"Do I have Laura LaForce on the phone?"

"Yes."

"Are you safe?"

"Yes."

"Can you tell me where you are?"

"I'm at a women's shelter."

"What's the address?"

"Sorry, I can't tell you."

"What happened? Can you tell me why you went missing?"

"Derek has been angry and out of control. He has severe drug and alcohol issues. I was scared of him overpowering me. Telling Derek goodbye would have been a dangerous move."

"I see. Is there a number you can be reached at?"

"Yes, and I provided the number."

"If I was to call you two days from now, are you still going to be there?"

"Probably, I don't know."

"Why?"

"This isn't a permanent residence. We're expected to find places of our own."

"Can I reach you at this number tomorrow?"

"Yes."

The next day at the court house, an emergency protection order was granted by the judge. I delivered the document to the police station. I was asked to take a seat and wait while an officer reviewed it.

"Laura, come with me. The sergeant wants to see you."

I quietly took a seat in an interview room. The door burst

open and a female cop entered. She made direct eye contact with me and aggressively slapped the table top. "What the hell's going on? How irresponsible! You should have told your husband you're leaving him," she snapped.

"My partner and I have been looking for you for days."

"If I had said good bye, you would have been tagging my remains instead."

"This isn't funny," she said, as she glared angrily at me.

The door slammed shut as she left the room. My stomach was in knots. I've never done well with confrontation. The door opened again, I waited, anticipating another verbal attack.

"Hi Laura, I'm Sergeant Craig. I understand you met my constable."

"Yes."

"I read the documents from the court house. I have questions I need to ask you."

"Go ahead."

"I understand he's planning on killing a client."

"Yes."

"I understand there are unregistered weapons on the property. Do you know where he keeps them?"

"He recently finished dry-walling the garage walls and claimed to have hid them in the wall."

"Where does he keep his drugs?"

"He keeps his drugs in the tool crib in the garage."

"What kind of drugs are there."

"Pot, hash, oil and whatever else he happens to be using. He's used acid in the past."

"I understand he was lying naked on a child's bed a while ago. Was that child sexually assaulted?"

"No."

The door opened and another officer entered the room.

"Have you been introduced to Constable Johnson?" the Sergeant asked.

"No," I responded.

"Hello," said Constable Johnson.

"Hi," I nervously replied.

"Is there anything else that didn't make these papers?"

"Yes," I hesitantly replied.

"Well?"

"Derek recently exposed himself to my grandmother. While she was preparing a pot of tea, he snuck up behind her naked, claiming he had a treat for her."

"Anything else you have to tell me?"

"Last week he threatened me with a sledgehammer after I poured his beer down the drain."

"I'll be back in a minute." the sergeant said. He stood up and left the room.

"Laura, you're very lucky to have escaped unharmed. I've come across women in your situation. They are either suffering from serious injuries or dead. I'm sorry about how harshly my sergeant is treating you. I'm not allowed to interrupt his questioning. If you need anything call me later. Here's my card," Constable Johnson said.

The door swung open and the loud intimidating sergeant was back.

"Laura were you ever going to tell us about any of this?"

The sergeant asked in an aggressive manner.

"Yes, I just didn't know when or how."

"What took you so long?" the sergeant's voice started to get louder.

"I was scared," I replied. I could feel my insides start to quiver with fear. The louder he got the worse it was.

"Did you ever call the police on Derek?" he impatiently questioned.
"No," I responded, while fighting back tears.

"Did you ever think about having any of these incidents recorded?" he asked in a serious manner.

"No, I was more concerned with my safety," I responded.

"You may go. I'll be contacting you if I have more questions." the sergeant said.

Later the same evening I received a call from the sergeant, informing me no weapons or drugs were found. I was asked to provide names and numbers of people who could verify the guns. Within an hour I received a call back from the police after they verified his guns. The sergeant wanted to know where I thought he might have relocated his guns.

I could hear Mary Ellen whisper "brother."

"Thanks, Mary Ellen."

"Try his brother Darcy."

The next morning I met my lawyer. We reviewed the facts and prepared for court the following day. Derek and his lawyer would also be attending.

His lawyer requested a discovery during morning chambers. Days later the discovery took place. I noticed after reading Derek's affidavit, that he was notified of a looming police search through his cheesy lawyer. While questioning me, she started asking a variety of questions about Derek's guns.

Suddenly a vision came to me right in the middle of discovery. The vision revealed Derek and Darcy on the phone in cahoots with each other over the guns. Derek had shipped Darcy the guns, by the Country Coach Bus Lines.

"Laura, did you hear my last question?"

"Can you please rephrase it for me?"

"Do you know where the guns are?"

"Darcy has them. Derek shipped the guns to his brother by bus." Derek looked mortified.

His lawyer started grasping for straws and asking inappropriate questioning about my menstrual cycle. Then she started asking who the cat belonged to. I became tired of her crazy questioning. I started to ask her questions out loud in sync with her and supply the answer with it. This was more than she could handle. Spit started flying from her quivering lips, as she stated, "I have no more questions."

After leaving the discovery hearing, I drove with my lawyer back to his office.

"You were phenomenal. You put her on edge. I've never seen anyone conduct themselves that way with her."

"Thanks, it didn't feel that way."

I headed back to the shelter. It was activity night and the women staying at the shelter knew I was a psychic. I was asked if I could do public group readings for the evening activity. Right away I obliged them.

I spent a good hour going around the circle revealing the good things each woman had to look forward to. Everyone was impressed with the accuracy. Even some of the staff had joined in.

The next day, just after leaving the shelter, I noticed three people stalking me. One of them resembled Veronica. I was so stressed my eyes were blurry and they felt like they were going to burst.

Upon returning to the shelter, I took a staff member aside and said, "I'm being followed."

"You've been through a lot lately. Sometimes when we're under stress the imagination can run wild."

"No, please listen to me. When I went out earlier today, three people rushed from around the corner of the house across the street. There were two guys and one female. They climbed into a white truck and followed me. I eventually lost them. The female resembled Veronica, a mutual friend of ours. She used to sit on the board of directors for the woman's shelter. Veronica has been in trouble lately."

"Laura, I think you're overreacting, if it happens again let us know. You should ditch that orange car. It stands out like a beacon."

Right away I called the dealership looking for Dina.

"Hi, Dina. This is Laura LaForce. Remember I recently contacted you about trading in my orange car for the navy blue vehicle I described."

"Yes, how is everything?"

"I did end up being in a hit and run, shortly after we spoke. I have just recently left my dangerous husband. I've been told to ditch this orange vehicle immediately."

"Can you call me back in an hour?"

"Sure."

An hour later I called Dina back.

"I have a navy blue PT Cruiser. Can you drop by and take it for a spin?"

"Dina, I'm going to be in a rush, can the paperwork be ready to sign? I'm kind of on the run. I don't stay in one place too long. Can you have the vehicle ready to go in an hour?"

"We'll try."

"Dina, it would make my situation easier."

An hour later I was at the dealership. While the sale was being processed, I sat waiting in a sales office. I closed my burning stressed eyes for a moment. A vision was revealed of Veronica and Derek having sex.

I went out for a drive later that afternoon. There was a rental poster in the window of a nice small townhouse. I called the number from my cell. The landlord met up with me ten minutes later. The place was clean, spacious and bright. The townhouse had two decks with glass doors and a beautiful landscaped yard. There was a laneway outside the gated fence. Many paths surrounded the townhouse in a park like setting. After viewing the place I arranged to sign the lease, the following day.

The next morning I sat with a social worker going over finances.

"That rent is a little high. Can you really afford this?"

"I'm not going to live in a dive. I can have my dog there."

"Are you sure?"

"Yes."

"Laura of all the ladies currently in this shelter, you're going to make it. You're even reluctant to take money from us. You can be on assistance for six months, possibly longer with what you've been through."

"Thank you, but you don't understand. I don't want this for myself. I grew up on welfare. I remember a time when the money ran out. We only had oatmeal to eat and water to drink for the entire week. There was no such thing as the food bank. Hopefully, I only need assistance for this month."

"My only concern at the moment is you're well being. Don't be surprised if you come down physically ill after the stress passes. Laura, we'll provide the damage deposit. The first cheque will have to cover the first months rent. I am going to issue you an extra thousand dollars for fleeing violence. Use it where you see fit. Call these people on this card. They will provide a food hamper and furniture if available."

"Thank you," I said.

Chapter Seven

TORMENTED

I spent the day enjoying the new place. After lunch I ventured out to the local park, which was empty. I was lying on the park bench relaxing in the sun for about five minutes. Suddenly I heard Mary Ellen's voice warn,

"Sit up! Watch out!"

A car approaching the park had slowed down, making a sudden U turn. The car drove into the adjacent school yard facing me. Two minutes later, the car drove up along the curb. Two shady men occupied the vehicle. The passenger wore a bandana. The passenger was extending his arms out the car window pointing a gun towards me.

I had managed to dial 911, while fleeing.

"911. How may I direct your call?"

"Police."

"What is the nature of your call?"

"Two guys drove up and pointed a gun towards me. They're driving around the outside of the school yard."

"Which school?"

"St. Emile's."

"What color is the car?"

"It's an older grey four-door car."
"Where are you?"

"I'm hiding behind the portables."

"There are two squad cars heading to assist you."

"What's your home address?" I gave him the address.

"You're close to home. Can I get you to head home? The squad cars are going to be circling the outside of the area.

"What if those guys are waiting for me there?"

"I'm sending a unit to your house. Where are you now?"

"In the field. I'm having trouble moving quickly. I'm recovering from injuries."

"Are you almost home?"

"I'm about five minutes away. I've just come to a street. Do you want me to take the path, sidewalk or parking lot?"

"Path."

Finally I arrived home. I was shaking, making it difficult to unlock the door.

"I'm home. Where are the police?"

"Lock your door and stay away from the windows. We'll be there in two minutes."

The police arrived seconds later.

"Officer, I recently left my abusive husband. I feel he is behind this. I know I'm stressed, but I suspect I'm being followed."

"What's your husband's full name?"

"Derek Napoleon Stevenson."

"What is his date of birth?"

"March 8th, 1946."

The officer brought Derek up on the computer.

"You're twenty years younger than Derek. He is not an upstanding citizen. He's been in and out of trouble for years. Five years ago was the last time we picked him up."

"What happened five years ago?"

"Sorry, I can't tell you due to the privacy act. He's just not good news. We didn't find the guys who were bothering you. There is a fifty percent chance your husband's involved. They could also be random drug dealers. Try not to worry. Call if anything else happens."

"I'm heading back to the women's shelter for the night."

A few days later I left the shelter, to live in the townhouse. A delivery truck arrived with a load of used furniture. I watched from the side lines as the men unloaded the donated items. Then, from the corner of my eye, I noticed movement some distance away at a utility box. A couple of heads randomly popped up and down from behind the box. 'Don't be silly! I told myself. It's probably neighborhood children playing.'

Nights later, while lying in bed with the window cracked open, I heard the back gate being unlatched, and the gate creak open. I could hear the dry crunchy autumn leaves being stepped on. Heavy footsteps climbed the wooden stairs of my deck. I could hear a chair leg scratch the deck floor as it was pulled. I heard a heavy body plunk down into the resin chair. A heavy cough pierced the night air followed by heavy breathing. Derek had arrived.

"God help me, Spirit protect me," I prayed.

I started to cough, which led to almost choking. I quietly rolled out of bed onto the floor. I grabbed my two pillows to put between me and the wall. I created a buffer zone for better protection in case he brought a gun. I was too scared to call the police. The idea of faking a call, in order to scare him off seemed better. If he was caught and released, I wouldn't be living long.

"Send the police, I've got a break and enter in progress." I said in loud voice.

Seconds later the gate slammed shut. I heard Derek's truck start the distance. I managed to peer out the window. He was in his truck, across the lane under a street light. Sickened at the sight of him, even at this distance, I shook uncontrollably as I watched him drive away. I stayed up the remainder of the night shaking in fear and vomiting profusely.

In the morning, I took out the garbage. While I was at the curb, a blue car slowed down as it approached. The driver briefly studied me. He resembled Derek's helper George. I felt uneasy. I went back inside my place and locked the door. I grabbed a cup of coffee, and headed to the living room to watch a talk show, hoping to distract myself.

Five minutes later a sudden thud rocked my place. I shook in horror as I got up to investigate. Beside the window was a five pound rock. The siding was dented. This stone hit the exterior wall, three feet away from where I had been sitting.

I called the police. Four hours later they arrived. While filling out the report, one of the officers tried to lighten the situation. He pleasantly smiled asking to be led to the offending rock. I took him outside and pointed to the rock beside the deck. I watch his jaw drop.

"Laura, that's not a rock. That's a lethal weapon. Show me where the rock hit the house and where you were sitting."

The officer's demeanor shifted. He silently matched the dent with the stone. He tried to figure out, where the rock was thrown from and sent his partner to grab an evidence bag. I asked if I could take a photo of the stone before they bagged it.

"If anything like this happens again call 911. Not the police dispatch line."

I was returning home later the following evening after running errands. I had just parked the car when I noticed the exterior house door was illuminated in orange. Spirit was warning me of a problem. Somebody had jimmied the locks. I tried to keep calm and unlocked the door. I was sensing negativity lurking close by. My stomach was in knots.

The next night I pulled into my driveway. I had just locked the car door. I was between the car and the townhouse. Three big guys were glaring at me as they rushed towards me. I raced up the stairs and fumbled to unlock the jimmied door in a panic. After getting in I locked the doors and raced to the bathroom sick with anxiety.
Later that evening things escalated. I was busy reading over some legal documents. Spirit had revealed dark grey silhouettes of four males surrounding my vehicle. I looked out my window to find two guys squatting on each side of my car facing towards the house. I immediately opened my door.

"Get out of here!" I yelled. The four left immediately.

I set my home alarm after closing the door. If things escalated, all I had to do was press the panic button on my keychain.

I called 911. This dispatcher had answered my previous calls, and minimized my situation. "It's probably kids playing." He told me.

"I'm putting you through to regular dispatch."

Ten minutes later, a full size barrel planter with plants was hurled at my parked vehicle. Right away I called 911 again, to explain things were escalating. Again he patched my call through to regular police dispatch. In desperation I pressed the panic button and let the alarm blare. The police were there within minutes, but were unable to find or catch the guys.

"Laura, I was on an important call, when yours was dispatched. I've been here a couple times and I always come up empty handed. I'm going to tell on you. I'm going to report you to my Sergeant." Constable Scott stated.

"I hate telling on others. Somehow, I always seem get into trouble, instead of 'the culprit.' I realize you're frustrated with my situation. Right now I have more to lose than you do. My life is at risk. I'm going to go speak with your Sergeant myself, in the morning." I replied.

I went to the police station first thing in the morning. I was led into the Sergeant's office to speak with him and his rookie Marissa.

"Laura, I understand the police were called to your place again last night. My constable didn't see or catch anyone. Is that correct?" he asked.

"Yes," I responded.

"How many times have you called the police lately?"

"Several," I answered.

"Please print out a record of every time Laura LaForce has called the police and bring it to me," he ordered his rookie.

Within minutes Marissa came back with a report and a huge smile on her face.

"Marissa, read me all the times Laura has called the police."

Marissa started reading the calls out loud from the list. The list included the dates, times and reason for the call. At the end, Marissa became elated as she announced "Psychiatric Assessment 1983."

She reacted as though she had solved a major crime. I could feel their energy shift, as looks were exchanged between the two of them. They both assumed I was mentally unstable. Finally the silence broke.

"Who's your family doctor?" the Sergeant asked.

"Dr. Anderson."

"I want you to go see him today. Tell him everything that's happened lately, hold back nothing. You seem to feel uneasy when I question you. I feel you'd be better off speaking with him. I'm going to call him and collect any further information directly from him." The Sergeant directed.

That horrific event happened when I was seventeen, over 22 years ago. It's now being thrown back in my face. I quietly got up and left in despair, my insides reeling in turmoil. I wished that someone had asked me why, instead of judging me and making assumptions.

Hours later, I saw my doctor. He was genuinely concerned about my situation. My body was extremely stressed. I had dropped 55 pounds in ten weeks. My stomach was physically sore to touch, my hair was falling out in clumps.

"Laura, your body is exhibiting signs of severe stress and fear. You look like you haven't slept in days. I'm very concerned for you and your safety. I know what Derek is like. I wouldn't want him after me. If there is anything I can do for you, let me know. If you die, I'll make sure your children are taken care of."

The following day, a detective from the spousal violence team called me to set up an interview. Waves of anxiety riveted through my body as I anticipated another interrogation. I knew anything I said could be twisted or perceived in a variety of different ways. If luck was on my side he would see the situation for what is was. Later that afternoon I met with Detective Tom Stevens.

"Laura, I ran both of your names through our system. Derek's a criminal with a stack of records. You don't have a record, but you were apprehended as a minor for running from a group home. I noticed that your husband is twenty years older than you. I've read reports indicating abuse. Can you explain to me how you ended up with him?" Detective Stevens leaned against the couch putting his arms behind his head waiting for my explanation.

"I met him at a party at a bar. We started dating and a short time later he asked me to move in with him on his acreage. One night he hurt me and I left. He kept telling me he was sorry and begged me to come back. I gave him another chance, but it wasn't long before the same issues resurfaced. I had enough and I was going to leave, but my financial situation was tight. I found an apartment and could only afford to put half the damage deposit down. On the way home my car was written off. The following week my birth control ran out and Derek refused to drive me into town to pick up a prescription. I tried using condoms, but he'd purposely lose them inside me. I ended up pregnant. I stayed hoping things would get better. I was threatened into marriage to make it right."

"Laura, I'm seeing control and abuse. Were you abused as a child?"

"Yes, many times."

"Unfortunately your past has led you to where you are today. When a young person is abused it becomes acceptable even though it's not. When the self esteem is low it's easier to become involved in abusive relationships. Do you understand?" Tom explained with a compassionate look on his face.

"Yes"

"He has lots of people after you. Do you know any of them? We need to have their names." Tom asked.

"I thought I spotted Veronica Brown following me from the women's shelter. One of the guys looked like George Farmer my husbands helper, but I didn't' recognize the car he was driving. My eyes have been so blurry from stress that it's hard to focus properly. There are sixteen male strangers involved who are all bigger than me. These guys are showing up in groups of two, three and four. There are several different vehicles involved." I sat trying to contain myself as tears trickled down my cheeks. "Several nights back I received a phone call on my new number with a muffled voice that sounded like Derek's saying 'get out, get out, get out.' Someone has access to my personal information."

"Why is it that you never told on him until recently?"

"Last year I was threatened by a couple of mobsters. I stayed in the marriage, because I feared for my life. These guys are very dangerous. One of them is in jail for the murder of a neighborhood man."

"Thank you for honesty. Our biggest problem right now is going to be getting Derek to back down. In his mind he sees you as a possession, which can be a dangerous situation. He's a mentally unstable alcoholic, who's addicted to drugs. He's an experienced criminal. He knows how to manipulate the system. We're going to put your address in our system as a point of interest and 911 priority. There is a chance that we might have to relocate you. I understand you're going through a divorce, you might want to consider letting him keep everything for your safety." Detective Tom's tone was extremely serious. "You can always replace your belongings, but you can't get your life back. Understand?"

"Yes"

"Laura, we've run out of time. We'll have to stop the session and continue tomorrow afternoon at the same time. If anything happens after hours call 911 and give them this file number when they arrive." Tom stood up passing me a card before showing me out.

While trying to relax at home that evening, I could sense the unsettling energy of a looming attack. I received a vision from spirit of a group of thugs gathering in the lane, another one was gathering across the way and a car with three people. The number sixteen was reveal.

"Holy shit" I gasped, "Sixteen against one." I quickly grabbed my jacket and purse, but in a panic I couldn't find the keys. "Where the hell did I put my keys?" Frantically searching every orifice of my purse, I finally found them in the bottom. Before I could get to the door my phone rang.

"Hi Laura, its Trudy, I just had a vision. Watch your back, they're after you. What are you doing?"

"I'm hitting the road right now."

"Oh my God, Laura be careful. Let me know if I can help."

The parking lot was clear as I drove away, but several blocks down the road a dark sedan stared to follow, which eventually led into a chase down the freeway. The stranger attempted to ram my rear bumper. Then he sped along side of my vehicle looking at me. Then he'd attempt to hit the side of my car. I fought to keep the car on the road as I dialed 911. I firmly held the cell phone against the steering wheel. I hollered for help, naming the landmarks as I sped down the freeway. Minutes later the guy decided to flee ahead of me. I kept up the pace long enough to shout his entire license plate into the phone. The police charged the thug with road rage, because they could prove an absolute connection to Derek.

The following day, two officers drove me in a paddy wagon to my place to pick up some belongings. Social services provided emergency funds for an immediate move, with the condition that my address was sealed. Nobody but my worker and specialized team were to know my whereabouts. The police put out an all points bulletin on Derek.

Chapter Eight

THE COURTS

The Vision

A couple days before divorce court, Spirit displayed Derek in my apartment corridor. Derek's hand was clenching a black-handled weapon. The remainder of the weapon was hidden under his jacket. Right away I was panic stricken, but hoping this was a knife, instead of a gun.

I called my worker Nancy and shared the vision with her. She was well versed with my abilities. Immediately uniformed security guards were arranged to escort and accompany me during court. A bodyguard would also attend my residence on those days.

I received a phone call the next day from Neva, a relocation program. Personal information was gathered during the interview to open a file. I was informed ahead of time not to say goodbye to family or friends.

The Judgment Room

Later that afternoon, I went to visit my friend Brenda, who was a psychic herself.

"The legal system doesn't seem to work for you. If I were you, I'd use your gift and take care of the situation," Brenda said with sympathy.

"What do you mean?"

"One time this guy hurt me. I wanted him to experience pain. I focused intensely on his right arm. A week later I saw him in a public place with the cast on that arm. He looked at me, then at his arm and ran."

"You intentionally manipulated energy to harm him? You attacked him on a psychic level. Am I right?"

"Yes."

"Was it easy to do?"

"Very easy, you know how we can take away pain. We can also inflict it."

"It makes sense. I had never thought of doing that."

I was feeling desperate and needed the whole situation with Derek to stop.

After spending hours thinking about the information Brenda shared earlier, I decided to give it a whirl before going to bed. I had nothing to lose.

My goal was to drain the energy from every single cell in Derek's body. With great anticipation, I laid on my back on top of my bed. After making myself comfortable, I surrounded my body with light for protection. Breathing deeply I focused on my mission. I prepared to astral travel out of my body. My spiritual body suddenly levitated two feet above the bed.

Seconds later, I found myself in Heaven, in the Justice Room. This is where serious matters are dealt with. The tiny room easily resembled one of our court rooms, with dark wooden benches and walls. The room could comfortably hold six people. There were only three benches, each three feet long, sitting one in front of the other. A small podium was at the front of the room. Off to the side was a wooden cubicle, occupied by a beautiful dark haired woman, dressed in black, wearing dark rimmed glasses. She seemed to be in her 40s.

Two other gorgeous angelic looking females in black robes also attended the room. A session was being reviewed. It was regarding Derek, who was severely tormenting me. The events were telepathic, visual and physical.

Derek's negativity was displayed through energy. His eyes were wide open like a zombie and his breathing was heavy. I understood through telepathy that he will be spiritually restricted after passing; until his soul is rehabilitated and restored or discarded.

I understood through telepathic energy, that I was to never do this again. This is considered a violation of spiritual power.

Derek was handcuffed in front and his ankles were shackled. Even though cuffed, he was forced to carry two huge books. The white book was the book of life and the black book was the book of death. Two umbilical like cords were placed on top of the books, one black and one white. These were the cord of life and the cord of death. Derek was led away to be contained. As he passed by me I started to vomit.

I woke on my own bed, choking on vomit and trying to catch my breath. I understood the severity of my actions. I will never partake that way again. Derek's punishment would be up to Spirit, not me.

The Testimony

I was back in court the following day to testify as a witness. I provided the details of Derek's death threats towards Dale to the courts. The judge seemed concerned and disgusted, as he heard the details.

The Past Life Regression

I decided to attempt a past life regression. Our souls retain important details from previous lives. In desperation, I requested to be shown a past life, which was relevant to my current circumstances. This took about three weeks to accomplish. The first couple of times, I bolted out of bed sweating with fear, but couldn't have told you why.

The last three regressions revealed some interesting facts from my past life. I could feel intense negative energy, even though nothing could be seen. Screaming and hollering and the sound of galloping horses filled the air.

The last dream brought perspective into my life. I was riding in a cavalry during a war. Spears were being thrown about. Derek was on a horse dressed as a bishop. Somebody riding behind me hollered, "Give him the power." I left, galloping off with a brown, leather-bound book. Derek and I had control issues stemming from a past life.

The Fraud

Intuitively I knew Derek wasn't finished tormenting me. Devastation loomed, but I didn't know how. In hopes of safety, I relinquished my rights to the house and other assets. Weeks later, I received a hefty bill from the government, which was immediately reversed. Derek had fraudulently used my social insurance number. In a moment of frustration I called on Mary Ellen.

"Is this fraudulent deed the devastation I was sensing?" Right away I was shown,

"No."

"What else is this bastard capable of?" I asked Mary Ellen through telepathy.

Everything went black, which I didn't understand.

Earlier in the day, Derek had been harassing me again. Before meditating I asked Mary Ellen to help me. I needed to know if the difficulties were ever going to stop. While meditating, I fell asleep.

The Message

Squeaking wheels woke me from my sleep. Mary Ellen appeared riding a huge antique tricycle. The grass surrounding her was an autumn yellow. She halted and using the horn on the handle bars, she honked twice, then she turned her head and looked directly at me.

"She won't pay and he goes," she stated in a squeaky high pitched voice. This tone is due to the difference of vibrations between the two worlds.

This message "she won't pay and he goes." still confuses me. Who is she? Is she me, a friend, a lover, a client, a family member, a drug dealer or a stranger? Won't pay in what capacity? Is this regarding money, attention, respect, or debt in a criminal dealing? "And he goes where?" Does he die, leave town, go insane or move on? I really don't know. I can't tell you.

Mary Ellen went on to show two relatives of Derek's who've since passed. I'm guessing by putting the pieces together that "he goes" means death.

My interpretation of this knowledge is: A situation involving a female not paying takes place when the grass is yellow. This situation somehow results in his demise.

Mother's Final Straw

I was running from Derek to save my life and attending the courts. I called my mother. I needed to talk.

"All this bantering back and forth is interesting. Aren't you glad I kept your father away?" was all she could offer.

A while later, she was badgering me to attend a family event with people she had previously lied to, about me.

"If you don't go, I'll lie about why you're not there," she threatened.

"Go right ahead; you've done it in the past," I replied.

Months later, a message was left on my answering machine by one of my siblings. "We know you're going to be upset when you catch wind of this. We're going to throw a party for Derek and play up to him, so that he doesn't think were using him. It doesn't matter how you feel, we're going to do this anyways."

This devastating act of betrayal was the final straw. I've forgiven them, but I don't need anymore of their dysfunctional reoccurring behavior affecting my life. I won't allow anyone to repeatedly hurt me. I haven't spoken to family since.

Chapter Nine

REVELATIONS FROM SPIRIT

One afternoon, while relaxing on the couch, I was shown a white bungalow, situated in the country, landscaped with rock work. The door was flush with the ground. A huge bay window covered the wall to the left. A breezeway attached to the house, connected to an office that led to a shop.

A client of mine was leaving after a reading. It was autumn, I could hear leaves being raked. My client suddenly said to the man in the yard,

"Your wife is good at what she does."

He replied, "Thank-you," with a pleasant gentle voice. I could see a fairer skinned hand on the rake and the work jacket worn by the man.

I was a little miffed and muttered to myself in utter disproval. 'I wasn't married to anyone.'

"Perhaps he was hired help, a contractor, or a neighbor, but nothing else. Single and safe was my comfort zone. I was disturbed by this for many months. I wasn't ready or willing to see or hear any of this."

A few evenings later, I was shown people quickly evacuating my apartment building and standing outside. I could hear alarms and see a fire truck. This vision appeared like a movie. I quickly observed and kept it in mind. Twelve hours later I was awakened by alarms. I quickly evacuated the premises and stood outside in the cold windstorm. My housecoat was blowing in the wind, as I stood outside with the others, waiting for help.

While waiting for the fire department, a neighbor offered me the warmth of his vehicle.

"Thank you for allowing me to sit in your warm car."

"You're more than welcome. I'm James."

"I'm Laura."

A few minutes later my stomach went into spasm, causing pain.

"Are you okay?"

"I'll be fine, it just doesn't feel great," I tried to keep my composure.

"There is an ambulance behind the fire trucks. I'm sure they wouldn't mind seeing you. They're sitting there doing nothing. Can I ask them to help you?"

"No."

"Why?"

"I'm in hiding, and under police protection. If they assist me my address will become public. The spasm will stop after awhile."

"I'm under police protection also."

"Why?"

"My wife tried to kill me. What about yourself?"

"My ex-husband, a friend and eleven strangers have been stalking and tormenting me."

"Are you the Laura who called into the radio talk show yesterday morning about family violence?"

"Yes."

"I heard you and the other two callers. Your stories were horrifying and overwhelming. This brought my situation to the surface and I ended up bawling!"

The fire department eventually allowed the residents in again. A group of neighbors decided to have coffee together. Upon parting James shook my hand.

"You should drop by for coffee again some time." Right away I heard Spirit blurt out, "Fat chance." What did this mean?

James and I shared many coffees. Several times while visiting an orb of an elderly lady would appear. She wanted to tell him she was okay. James was uneasy with the idea of me being a medium. I didn't want to push him beyond his comfort zone. I never relayed her message and maybe I should have.

One evening while visiting, James opened up.

"I had an accident a couple years ago, an elderly woman in the other vehicle died. My life hasn't been the same since, I live with this everyday. I never wanted to kill anyone."

"What happened?"

"I was driving a semi on highway 44 and her Toyota blew the stop sign. Everything went into slow motion. I tried to stop the truck. She was pronounced dead at the scene."

"I'm sorry that happened to you. If you ever need to talk I'm here."

As he spoke, I remembered seeing this accident on the 5 o'clock news. After viewing the fatal accident, I had judged him harshly as a worthless, careless trucker.

Before parting for the night James mentioned, "It would be nice to spend more time together."

"James, it would be nice to spend more time together, but just for now, nothing serious. I have no future plans for a man in my life. I don't think I'm capable of loving again. I hope you understand."

"I'm pretty much on the same page," he said.

After arriving home, I received a vision of James sitting on his couch. He was flailing his arms about, while speaking with an angry look on his face.

Two nights later we were having a coffee together. The vision unfolded before my eyes.

"I'm really angry with my ex-wife. She has everything I worked hard for. I can't even see my children." As he spoke I closed my eyes. I saw two lit-up youths in his company.

"Your children are going to return shortly."

"Can you torment her through voodoo?" he asked as he flailed his arms about in anger.

"No."

"Why?"

"I don't practice voodoo. It would be a misuse of power."

James and I started spending more time together. After a couple of exchanges of affection, I started to have feelings for the man.

One night while visiting James, he left the room to grab us another coffee. I quickly closed my eyes "Spirit, show me this time next year." Immediately I received a vision of an operating room.

"No Dan, I didn't ask to see an operating room. I want to know about my relationship with James next September."

Everything went black. That was really odd, Dan displaying an operating room. "Is James healthy?" "Y", which means yes was drawn midair, "Dan, I don't know why you're holding out on me. Can you show me something I can relate to?" Nothing more was shared.

Gradually the time spent with James lessened. Most of my time was spent missing him. I hounded Dan for answers.

"Dan, will James come around tonight?"

Upon closing my eyes, I was shown two monochrome figures embracing. This display always meant yes.

"What time will I see him?"

A number ten was shown as our meeting time.

"Do I call him?" Letter "Y" meaning yes was displayed.

I called James and we had coffee.

The next day the same scenario of questioning took place.

"Dan, will I see James tonight?"

I saw nothing, which meant no.

"Will James at least call tonight?

Again I saw nothing.

"Can you somehow force James to call me?"

Dan yawned and walked away, right in front of me. He was tired of this and I was desperate.

Days later, while clearing a client's home, a sudden thud came from the stairwell. I went to investigate. On the stairs was a wall hanging of a poem, which had fallen. Something interesting caught my eye. I decided to read it. It spoke of a few good people, honest and loving. The poem spoke of having courage and wisdom to carry on. This verified what I already knew and moved me to the point of tears.

Spirit went to great lengths trying to show me that James wasn't the one. I was shown his wedding day, with a different woman on his arm. This didn't affect me. I had no plans of ever marrying again.

Mary Ellen went to the point of literally proving his lack of interest. I was walking down a stairwell and heard footsteps behind me.

"Look behind you," ordered Mary Ellen. I looked behind me to discover James. He had a scowl on his face.

"Excuse me," he said as he brushed by, treating me like a stranger.

Not having the time of day or the courtesy to say hello, he was probably having a bad day, I reasoned. There would be other times for us to visit.

A couple weeks later, while sharing a morning coffee with James, I could see him losing his job. I didn't dare tell him. Being the bearer of bad news is not rewarding.

Later that afternoon, I was shown a vision of myself sitting alone on my sofa. I knew within a short period of time, James was no longer going to be part of my life. The feelings of anguish and grief were overwhelming. My heart started to throb.

"Dan or Mary Ellen, please reverse this situation?" I begged. "I don't want to lose James. Show me a sign that I can understand. Somebody do something please."

Feeling desperate I decided to start my Christmas shopping. James loved burning candles. I bought him a large cylinder shaped beige vanilla scented candle. I found a beautiful orange square dish to compliment it.

After returning home I decide to give James a quick call.

"Hi James, how are you doing?"

"I just lost my job." he said in a despairing voice.

"Would you like to discuss what happened over coffee?"

"No, I don't want to see anyone. I just want to run away."

"Can I run away with you?"

"Laura, of all people, you should know that running away is done alone." he replied in a loud angry voice.

"I'm sorry James. I've been missing you."

"I need time to myself. I want to be alone."

I was upset and I decided to go for a walk in the cool evening air. I noticed in a distance, James was cleaning out his vehicle. Suddenly a shooting star was tumbling from the heavens over the parking lot. I only wished "for a little longer with James."

When I returned from my walk, my friend Tony called, desperately needing to see me. He arrived, looking worn and extremely upset. I made us a cup of tea and we settled into the living room to talk.

"What's bothering you Tony?"

"Laura, I'm very scared of dying. I'm terrified of the consequences. In my 43 years of life. I haven't been a very nice person. I became a gangster and hurt many people, putting a few in wheelchairs. Their lives were ruined because of me. Dying would be easier if I hadn't done these things. I pray to God every night, begging for forgiveness."

"What is it that you fear the most?"

"Going to hell and burning for eternity."

"A destructive soul is segregated; rehabilitated or cut out."

"How do you know?"

"I was shown. Plus I've been to the other side."

"You've been there?"

"Through astral travel I've had some access."

"What was it like?"

"The other side is beautiful and peaceful. Heaven is spiritual, not material. The sunrise I encountered was breathtaking. Green lush grass covered the grounds and parks. The buildings resembled old Greek and Roman structures.

My access was limited. Each of the four times I was on the other side, I was either alone or with my Spirit Guide. Most communication was telepathic. I wasn't able to visit with the deceased in heaven, because I'm not dead.

"Do you think I'll be okay?"

"In the past while you've been doing good deeds for others. You realize how badly you affected others. Being sincerely sorry should have some benefits. You won't end up with a great reward for past behavior, but I think you'll be okay."

"Thanks Laura, you helped ease my worries. I better go home it's getting late."

"Have yourself a good sleep, you need it." I said, giving Tony a hug before he left.

Chapter Ten

THE CAPRI

One evening while watching TV, I received a vision of a stranger on the verge of committing suicide. This information was extremely upsetting. Even worse, I didn't know this person or how to find him. How was I to help? I really wasn't ready to deal with this sort of situation. This disturbed me for the remainder of the night. I needed my rest. I was scheduled for readings the next day at the Capri Restaurant.

After arriving at the restaurant, I settled in for the day. As I was preparing to start work, I shut my eyes. The white viewing screen, which I see when I'm working with my third eye, was gone. This was replaced by a huge field, with an old fashioned tap and pumped handle. Eventually, a big water drop hung off the edge of this tap. After the drop fell, my white screen returned and information flowed like wildfire.

I shared this with Jack, another psychic at the Capri, during break.

"Laura, you've tapped into the field of knowledge. You have what the other psychics working here don't have. Many are jealous of your ability. You won't be here much longer. I see you becoming a predominant psychic, the next Madam."

After coffee a young man in a cap quickly seated himself at my table.

"Sir, you must wait your turn," the waitress stated as she forcefully led him away by his arm.

"Lady, please let me talk to her," he replied.

A mother with a little girl was ushered in to see me. "I don't know if you see children, but I'd like you to see her."

"I don't mind, I like children."

"Mom," the little girl interrupted "Why are we here?"

"To visit Laura" she replied.

Right away I directed my attention to the child.

"I'm Laura, What is your name?"

"Becky."

"How old are you?"

"Three."

"What is your mom's name?"

"Kate, but I have to call her Mom."

"It's nice to call her Mom" I replied.

"I used to be her mom and I liked that more."

"But now it's her turn to be the mom." I answered.

"Becky keeps doing this to me. She even tries to run the household, she claims that she's lived longer and knows more. Last night I was bathing her. She stopped splashing around and made direct eye contact, telling me, 'I used to be your mother.' She often refers to me as her young one."

Becky sat enjoying the rocks displayed on the table.

"Which rocks do you like and why?"

Becky quickly divided the rocks into two piles. "These are everyday outside rocks." She pointed to the pile.

"These ones are special, they make you feel good."
Becky grabbed the tarot deck and started looking through them.

"Becky, don't get into Laura's things," Kate demanded.

"They're only cards," Becky exclaimed.

"You're right Becky," I told her.

I handed Becky an angel deck.

"What do you think of these?" I asked Becky.

Seconds later a big smile appeared on her face. Becky had pulled a card of a native woman without wings.

"This one is real," she stated. "I used to look like her."

"Who's having a baby?" I asked.

"Auntie Brenda," she answered in excitement. Kate's jaw dropped.

"Becky, how do you know? Nobody's supposed to know."

"There's a tiny baby boy in Auntie's stomach."

"Please don't tell anybody else," she begged Becky.

"Who's getting married?" I asked. Right away she pointed her finger at me and replied,

"You are."

"Kate, Becky is an old soul. She was your mother in a previous life."

"Becky used to stare and contently coo at the air, shortly after my mother passed. Did my mother appear to her?"

"It is very common for loved ones and ghosts to appear to young children. Children are very open to the spirit world."

"What about Becky's invisible friend, who she constantly interacts with?"

"She's communicating with her spirit guide through play, in the form of a playmate," I said, before explaining more details to her.

Usually as children mature, they start to close themselves off, due to this being somehow, unacceptable. Other times, parents discourage their participation. Just like speaking another language, they gradually lose their tongue.

Many children coming in are old souls. They are psychic and sensitive. These children are spiritually advanced and have outstanding abilities. These children are our future. They deserve to be heard, loved, and respected.

The Desperate Stranger
The waitress finally led the desperate man to my table. He immediately seated himself.

"Young man, please remove your cap," I demanded.

After removing his cap, I recognized him right away as the suicidal male, the one I had been shown last night. I wished I had training in dealing with these circumstances.

I took a couple of deep breaths before starting the reading session. I needed to be grounded and calm. I quietly called on my spirit guides and the young man's spirit guide also. Dan instructed me to be gentle and direct.

"Hello, I am Laura. Could I have your name please," I asked. "Matthew," he mumbled.

"Matthew, at quarter past eight last night life was unbearable. You were ready to kill yourself, but backed out

120

at the last minute."

Matthew burst into tears and sat sobbing uncontrollably. This was a huge release for him. I could feel the negativity coming to the surface. I waited for him to settle down before continuing on. I held his hands to keep him with me.

"You suffer from depression and anxiety. As a boy, your father beat you many times with his fists. One day your father, in a drunken rage, struck you across your face with his belt leaving huge welt marks. A neighbor noticed the marks and called the police. A lady from Social Services took you away. You were six. You spent many years as a loner."

Matthew started shaking at this point. He was in total meltdown, but safe. After a few minutes he started to calm down.

"I have no friends. I'm scared of everything. My food's contaminated. There are germs on everything. I'm afraid of getting sick and dying. I have to wash my hands all the time and I have nightmares."

"What do you enjoy, Matthew?" I asked.

"Nothing, I wish I were dead," he replied.

"What would happen if you got sick?" I asked.

"I might die."

"What if you died, then what?"

"I don't know! Maybe somebody would bury me."

"Where would you be?"

"Dead in the ground."

"Matthew, if you died, your soul would go to Heaven. Only

your body would be placed in the ground. The human body is like an egg shell: after we're finished with the body, it is discarded. Our energy is like egg whites, with or without the outer shell the energy exists. The soul is similar to the egg yolk. The egg yolk holds its shape without the shell or the egg whites. At the moment of death the shell releases the soul and the energy which sustained bodily life."

"How many times have you been sick from eating contaminated food?" I asked.

"None, I guess," he replied.

"There are many germs on all sorts of things. How many times have they made you deathly ill?"

"Never." he answered.

"People become depressed after experiencing many terrible things like you have. Then anxiety sets in. This is what is happening to you. With professional help and work on your part you can overcome this and have a good life. Can I give you a number to call for help?" I asked.

"Yes," he replied.

I found the number for the Mental Health Association and wrote it on my business card.

"They are free and can help you."

"Can I share a couple of neat things I see happening for you?" I asked.

"Sure," he replied.
"I see you finishing high school. Afterwards you'll take a course in auto mechanics. At first you'll work for a dealership servicing vehicles. Later you'll find your way into restoring antique vehicles. You even rebuild one for yourself and paint it red."

"That sounds okay."

"About five years down the road you'll meet a young lady. You're very hesitant and shy at first. She is very good to you and has had her own hardships."

"Will I marry her?" he asked.

I closed my eyes and went to Spirit looking for the approval, everything lit up.

"Yes, Matthew, you marry her."

After I finished his reading, the waitress approached me.

"You took too long with him. You made him cry."

"He was in need, please let me be."

Nothing else was said.

War by Invasion

I received a premonition of a war during a reading. Immediately I relayed the news to my client.

"Abdul, there is going to be an uprising where you live. I'm seeing gangs fighting in the street. The Christians are being attacked. Houses are being set on fire. Some of the legal authorities are tied in with them. Two very threatening people will be standing outside your door. You're going to be leaving with only the clothes on your back," I warned him.

"My home has never been a war zone. Are you sure?" he replied.

"I see this happening within the month."

"Will I have a home to return to afterwards?"

"Yes."

This situation occurred three weeks later in Maghar, Israel near the Sea of Galilee. Peace has since been restored and Abdul is now safely home.

Husband Apologizes

Minutes later, a woman was seated across from me.

"Laura, I think you're a little young to be reading me. Most of the readers in are over forty"

"How old do you think I am?"

"I would say you're between thirty three to thirty five years old."

"I wish you were right. I recently turned forty." The lady's jaw dropped.

"Do you still want a reading from me?"

"I'll give you a chance."

I shut my eyes before starting her session. In my third eye, a vision started unfolding. There was a darker bearded male approximately forty years of age. He was standing on a bar stool with the noose around his neck, which was tied to a rafter. Suddenly he jumped off the stool. His head hung differently and his body swung for short while.

"I'm sorry. I love you," he lip-synched.
The whole situation was sickening. I opened my eyes while panicking, on the verge of vomiting. Jack came running with a garbage can, after witnessing this.

"I'm sorry. I need a few moments to collect myself."

After a few minutes, I described the details of what I'd seen to my client. Various emotions, including teary eyes, crossed my client's face.

124

"Thank you, Laura. My husband killed himself, four months ago. I needed this closure."

I needed a short break after this to regain my composure and had a quick coffee with Jack.

"Laura, you need to release what happened. Don't allow this to bother you."

Evil Entity

A well made-up pretty young woman with long blonde hair, wearing designer clothing, quietly took her seat across from me.

"May I please have your name?" I asked. "Candice."
We joined hands and I closed my eyes. A dark shaded entity resembling the devil appeared.

"Oh my God, help us," was all I could utter. An evil entity had a tight grasp on this young girl.

"You are being controlled by a very evil entity, one who currently lives in flesh. Your life is at risk. You need to get away now, before it's too late."

"I've tried. I can't," Candice cried.

"The man you're running from is evil, he's killed others. He'll kill you."
"He is my show manager. He's a pimp. I'm scared of him."

"You really should talk to the police," I mentioned.

"I can't, he'll find out," she cried.

"I understand you're terrified, but you need to leave town immediately. You can outrun him and save your life. You need to change your physical appearance. Take off your make up, go natural. Pull back or cut your hair; after you're safe, dye it. Put on a pair of jeans and a sweatshirt. Wear nothing that draws attention to you. Plain Jane blends with the public."

"Where do I go?" she asked.

I closed my eyes and went to Spirit. I was shown "W".

"Catch a bus out of town this afternoon and head west. Tell nobody that you're leaving and don't come back for at least five years."

"Am I going to be okay?" She hesitantly inquired. I closed my eyes and went to Spirit.

"Yes, as long as you leave today." I replied.

Later in the day, a rough looking male about 24, sat down to be read. Negative energy dominated his whole aura. An open wound appeared at the upper side of his head, through recently shaved hair. It was almost as if a bullet had grazed his head. I silently asked for protection, before proceeding with his reading.

"Can I ask your name, please?" I asked.

"Charles," he replied.

I shut my eyes and went to Spirit without touching his hands. Everything went pitch black. After a while I was shown drug issues, a stabbing, and a shooting. He buried a loved one, who died in his arms.

"Charles, it's a very bad time for you. Total devastation has come into your life. Your drug dealings have gone upside down and cost you a loved one."

Charles sat there on the verge of tears.

"They shot my girlfriend, she died in my arms. One of the bullets grazed my scalp."

"Your girlfriend took the bullet which was intended for you."

"I'm out on bail and have another hearing coming up. I'm being accused of shooting at the other party. Do you see me getting off?"

Charles was becoming angry and started to slightly lift and tilt the table towards me, while waiting for an answer.

"There are going to be some repercussions."

"Why? I never shot anyone."

"No? What about the guy you knifed, when you were high?"

"I don't remember, I don't remember." He started to cry.

"Are things going to get better for me, if I change?"

"Charles, you need to make many changes in order to find peace and restore happiness. This means finding new friends and completely leaving the drug trade. This will be your choice. It's completely up to you."

After a long day at the Capri, it was finally time to go home. As I drove down the cold icy winter highway, I kept hearing the horrific scream of a woman. This was repeatedly followed by a vision of a person bundled in winter clothing falling out of a moving vehicle. Later in the evening, I turned on the local news. A story was broadcast of a woman falling to her death, from a vehicle on the highway. This tragic event happened about an hour before I received the visions, on another highway close by where I was driving. The essence of this lady was earthbound and trying to reach out.

While driving my car the following morning, the sound of breaking glass shattered my nerves. I wondered if this was a warning of a car accident. A couple of days later, I heard the disturbing sound of breaking glass for the second time.

Two days later, it was the morning of my fortieth birthday. I gradually talked myself into going to work. I'd been cleaning people's houses for years and I was getting tired of it. My body hurt from the physical work. I look forward to the days when I could stop cleaning and survive on readings instead. I eventually arrived at my client's home to clean her house. I went to grab my client's vacuum cleaner from her basement. The sound of breaking glass echoed throughout the household.

"Is everything okay?" I hollered while running up the stairs.

"No, I split my head open," Annette screamed.

I felt sickened as I rushed upstairs to help her. She was sitting on the dining room floor, beside the chandelier, holding her head. Blood and shards of glass decorated the golden laminate floor. I grabbed a towel and applied pressure to her bleeding scalp.

"What happened?"

"I was cleaning the chandelier and it came crashing down on my head.

"Annette, I'll call for help. What is your address?" I asked.
"No, don't call anyone. I'm okay."

"You don't look fine, you're injured and in shock."
We were out of town on an acreage. To make things worse, I didn't know her address.

"If you call for help you're fired." She ordered. "You have the gift. Heal me."

"Gift does not replace first aid."

She wouldn't accept no for an answer.

"Annette, your neck and upper back are injured, you really need medical help." To me she looked very pale.

"No, I only hurt my head."

"Spirit, please help me keep Annette alive and the bleeding under control."

If she would only pass out, I could dial 911 for help. They would be able to trace her address to the phone number. I kept sending her healing energy. Every minute felt challenging, I felt like a hostage.

"Spirit, please help me. Surround her with your healing powers."

Three hours later, Annette finally gave in.

"I need to see a doctor, my neck and back are hurting. Laura, you don't look so great. I'm sorry, I drained you!"

This event left me sick for the next three days. On the third day I called my Reiki master and I told her what had happened. Right away she started working on things.

"Annette is still siphoning your energy. I need to cut the cords she has attached to you. Do you realize you kept her earthbound?"

"Yes, that was my intent."

"People can attach to you and drain you completely. She's literally sucked the life out of you. You need to rest and eat well over the next couple days. I will continue to reclaim your energy." It took me a couple days to recover.

Chapter Eleven

TWIST OF FATE

Sometimes challenging circumstances and hardships fall in our lives. These include: relationship breakdown, family chaos, an accident, illness, financial ruin or worse. These events help us to focus on what is important in life.

A prophetic dream revealed a serious accident. My navy car was struck by a green delivery truck in the front passenger's side panel. The car landed against a concrete wall near a bridge. Snow and water surrounded the scene. I was injured and stuck in my vehicle. A uniformed fireman was on the scene.

In prophetic dreams the receiver observes the event in color, much like a bystander. These dreams occur within minutes of falling asleep or before waking.

The accident was shown again, two nights later. I woke in a panic and tried to put the details together. "Watch out for green trucks, driving to your right. Stay away from bridges. Stay away from walls. Don't drive during sunrise or sunset." This should be easy enough to avoid.

I was enjoying my morning coffee at the kitchen table. A vision of three men was revealed midair. I recognized two of them as being my new office landlords. The third man was unknown to me. The large stranger stood smiling. Huge burn scars covered his face and arms.

"Are these men alright to deal with?"

I saw a flash of white light, which means fine or positive.

"Thank you, Spirit."

The morning was going to be busy. I was excited to be moving

my business from home into an office. I treated my friends Bill
and Tony to breakfast.

"Bill would you mind driving my car today? I've had two
dreams two days apart of a horrific accident. I'm deeply
concerned something could happen today. If you drive, we're
safe. You weren't in the dream."
We arrived at my new office with a truckload of furniture.
The landlords introduced me to a third partner. He was identical
to the stranger in the vision. We went on to move my
furnishings into the new office. Tonight was Nina's Christmas
party. I decided to wait a good twenty minutes after the sun
set, before heading out. I felt a little uneasy, but reassured
myself nothing would happen.

'It's dark outside now, everything should be fine,' I said to
myself.

There was lots of snow and mush on the road. Twenty
minutes later on the freeway, a green truck veered side
ways. The front of the truck connected with the passenger
panel of my car. My car came to a stop against the concrete
wall of the freeway.

This happened within a half block of an approaching
underpass bridge. Everything was identical to what I had been
shown.
I was badly injured and unable to move my legs. Thoughts of
panic raced through my head.
"Am I paralyzed? How am I going to get up to my office?"

The pain was severe. My body had gone into shock. A
firefighter arrived at the window.

"I'm Brad. What's your name?"

"Laura."

"Where are you hurt?"

"My legs and feet hurt really bad. I can't move them."

"How's your neck?"

"Tender."

"Keep still, more help is coming. I'm coming in to help you."

I could hear the firefighter crawl through the back of the car. Both his hands immobilized my head. A paramedic arrived at the window and she started to ask questions as she climbed in.

"I'm going to check you out; tell me if something hurts."

I remember nothing else, until I heard a piercing scream. This resulted from having my leg touched.

While being rescued from my vehicle, I felt apprehensive. My worst fear was the pain I might experience while being moved. I started floating in and out. The pain was only bad when I was there. I felt sudden warmth in my solar plexus area, which was peaceful and extremely inviting. I felt my body wanting to merge with the energy.

The minute rescuers loaded me into the ambulance, the paramedic attending me became very concerned.

"Would the driver come join us in the back," she firmly requested.

I heard a man's voice speaking with the driver, offering to drive the ambulance. "Are you sure you can drive this?" I heard him ask.

Another wave of warmth surfaced through my solar plexus on the way to hospital.

"Breathe," I heard both paramedics say loudly at the same time.

I was brought into the trauma room, immobilized on a backboard. I was surrounded by emergency room staff, as they assisted the doctor. This doctor seemed familiar, but I couldn't place her. Shortly before I was whisked off to x-ray, the police showed up.

"Can we see Laura LaForce?" a man's voice asked.

"We're going to be taking her to x-ray in a few minutes. Please make it quick, she isn't doing well. The painkillers should be taking affect soon," replied a nurse.

The one officer came up close to me. I was relieved, once I saw his face. He and his partner dealt with the five pound rock over a year ago. Thankfully this officer was kind and pleasant to deal with.

"Laura, can you talk for a minute?"

"Yes."

"What happened?"

"A truck hit my car on the freeway."

"What speed were you travelling?" "I don't remember."

"Was anything funny going on?"

"No, I wasn't being chased."

"I need to get some paperwork done. Can I leave the forms with you to be filled out? Can you get them back to me within the week?"

"Why don't you fill out the report and take it with you? I trust you."

"You'll sign it?"

"If you hold it up, I'll try my best."

He wrote the report himself. By then I was very drowsy from the painkiller.

"Laura I'm finished with the report, do you want me to read it to you before you sign?"

"No."

"I'm putting a pen in your hand to sign the report." He held up the form on a clipboard to my wrist and I signed it.

Minutes later, I was in the x-ray room, for what seemed to be a long time. While waiting for the x-ray results, I remained immobilized on a backboard. I was finally able to place this kind gentle emergency room doctor, who had been treating me very well. I recently read her at the Capri. I remembered her being extremely impressed with my abilities.

"Laura, I'm concerned about you. Your heart was acting funny when you first arrived, but has since settled down. Thankfully nothing is broken, but your pelvis and legs are badly injured. This is going to take time to heal. I'm going to send you home. If anything changes, come back immediately."

Chapter Twelve

THE GOLDEN HEART

While recovering from injuries and mourning James, my living room became my sanctuary, the place I would pray nightly for James. As a token of my love, I chose to use the candle I had bought him for Christmas. The candle had its place on the coffee table. With a steady hand and teary eyes, I would strike a match and light his candle.

"Spirit, I would like James back if at all possible. Bring him peace and happiness. Bring his children back into his life. Allow him a job he enjoys. Show him that he is loved. Please allow him to experience love with me."

By this point, I would be sobbing with tears running down my face. In exhaustion, I would lie back and allow my self to cry. On occasion, I would fall asleep crying.

I had been doing this for weeks. After a while, I heard through the grapevine one of his children had visited him. I was so pleased for him. That evening, I set the candle and dish on the kitchen table. In case I fell asleep while praying, nothing would be accidentally knocked over. I wondered what I was going to do with his candle when I moved.

I slowly approached my kitchen table and struck the match. I extended my hand, lit the candle, and bowed my head.

"Spirit, provide James with the love, respect, and attention he deserves. May he experience love and peace with or without me."

How could I utter the words "without me"?

I was shocked and overwhelmed with what had come out of my mouth. I bawled as I headed to the sofa to lie down. I cried myself to sleep.

My legs were stiff and hurting. I awoke in pain from sleeping in a scrunched up position. Looking at my watch, I had been sleeping only thirty minutes. The living room was dimly lit, and my kitchen was dark. Being half awake I grabbed my matches. I headed to the kitchen to relight his candle. The candle was gone.

The candle had melted all over the large square dish. Wax extended across my three foot rectangular table, forming an upside down letter "V". The lines which made up the "V" resembled uncrossed crossbones. The peak represents togetherness and the lines each go in a different direction indefinitely. I understood the answer and started to cry.

I sought the comfort of my couch, where James and I used to sit. As I sat sobbing, I was shown two black stickman carrying a black coffin. Seeing this, I realized Tony would be dead shortly.

Within seconds a huge solid golden heart was revealed. On each side of the heart were dark silhouettes. One woman and one man made for each other. They share the heart and the love forever. Warmth, love and tranquility filled the energy of the heart.

Within weeks, two golden heads were revealed touching at the forehead. The vision went from being a random sighting to a regular occurrence.

One day the two golden heads were blessed by a golden hand with the sign of the cross.

"Spirit this is crazy. There is nothing great or blessed going on in my life. All I seem to ever have is challenges and hardships. Show me something tangible, that I can at least grasp." Not everything revealed is meant for today.

A couple months after the accident, I could still hardly sit, stand or walk. I needed to figure out what to do with my office and its lease. The office I chose was no longer viable. It was on the third floor with no elevator. The stairs would be physically impossible.

"Dan, what am I going to do about my office?"

"My Navy PT cruiser was displayed travelling down a highway. Green grass filled the ditches. A decal was on the rear window."

The office wasn't meant to be. I was going to have to let it go. My business with Spirit was to be on the road. My car was now drivable, but snow was still on the ground. This would take place in the summer, but not necessarily this year. I still needed to recover from my injuries.
After spending months in physical therapy, my injuries were slowly improving. I needed to get past the frustration and anger before I could fully heal.

"Mary Ellen, it's been three months since the accident. These injuries need to heal. My life is limited by this. Relying on others is not what I call living. Why should I suffer because of someone else's mistake?"

Right away, I was shown a pair of white glowing hands resembling mittens. White illumination means healing on the spiritual plane. These lit hands would touch illuminated feet, one at a time. Next each foot was aggressively manipulated and shaken. Close to the scene was a stage with musical instruments. This was a message of healing but didn't make sense.

Later that evening my friend Tracy called needing a ride from the dance. After arriving in the parking lot, Tracy was nowhere in sight. This meant I would have to track her down, by going into the hall. I balked at the idea of a long painful walk.

Upon entering, a band was performing on the stage. Betty, a healer friend, was sitting with Tracy near the stage. After a slow painful walk, I arrived at their table.

"Hi, Laura."

"Hi, Betty."

"How are you doing?"

"I'm still struggling with the injuries."

"I heard about what happened to you. Sit down. Let me see your feet."

"Betty, the pelvis is injured."

"No, your feet had jammed into the ankles upon impact. Everything went upwards affecting your pelvis and lower back."

The whole scene revealed to me earlier unfolded in seconds. All details were exactly as I had been shown. The pain was excruciating as Betty put the feet and ankles back into position.

"You need to take something to reduce the inflammation for a week. Remember to ice both feet as well."

"Thank you, Betty."

I quietly bowed my head and thanked Spirit as well.

Chapter Thirteen

THE SERMON

I was heading out of town with my friend Tanya. We were making an attempt to visit her brother Scott whom she hadn't seen in years. Tanya was sick of Scott's wife, who literally controlled him. I understood he shared my ability. I really wanted to meet him.

"Laura, let me try calling him before we leave town," Tanya begged.

"Hi Scott, it's your sister Tanya. I'd really like to see you. We're heading your way this afternoon."

"Let me ask my wife." The phone was quiet for a minute.

"Hi Tanya, I won't be able to see you. We're going to be busy."

Tanya sadly hung up the phone. I sensed this was a lie to please his wife.

"We shouldn't go, she won't allow us see him. Gertrude, his wife, is a practicing witch you know."

"Why would that stop us from visiting?" I asked.

"She has power and control over the situation and she doesn't like me."

"I would really like to meet Scott. Let's go anyways. If we get turned away at least we tried. You have other brothers over there, which you haven't seen in a while."

"That's true."

Tanya and I started out on our journey. While driving it felt as if a bullet had hit my head. The sensation was so realistic. I felt my head to double check. Better safe than sorry! With all the drive by shootings, you just never know! A severe headache settled in and lasted for several hours.

Arriving in Calgary, I was immediately able to find the address, without a map. Usually I can get lost and turned around with a map. Arriving at the door, we were refused entry by Gertrude. While talking to us she was staring intently flicking her tongue on her two bottom front teeth. This made me feel uneasy. I knew she was up to something bad. Gertrude was definitely attempting to inflict negativity on us. I quickly shut my chakras down hoping to escape any negative impact.

Magic was something I actually doubted in the past. Today I know and realize this is real. I don't partake in it myself. In regard to witches, there are good and bad, just like the rest of us.

"Would you like to see your brother Brian?"

"That would be great, let's go see him."

Brian invited us to spend the night.

"Laura, are you planning on attending mass with us in the morning?" asked Tanya.

"No Tanya, I used to years ago."

"You were raised Catholic."

"I no longer practice the Catholic faith. I haven't for years."

"That's okay," piped up Brian. "Laura will have to sit through my dry Sunday morning sermon on divorce."

The others left to attend mass, while I stayed behind with Brian.

140

"Laura, I'm a retired United Minister. I'm like you. I practice my faith in the closet. I don't need anyone to go between me and the spirit of God. Let's go to the kitchen and we'll prepare our sermon."

We headed to the kitchen and he started to heat up his electric frying pan. "Why don't we make bacon and eggs for this morning's sermon?"

We sat chatting away, while enjoying breakfast together.

"Laura, I understand you're gifted. This has been in your family for many years. Everybody has tried to keep this quiet. They refer to it as the curse. I realize your ability is stronger than that of your ancestors. Be careful; others in the world are still naïve."

"I understand."

"What are your religious beliefs?" he asked.

"I believe Jesus was a psychic medium, who was sent by God from heaven to share spirituality. Jesus taught love, compassion, and healing. He demonstrated the power of the Holy Spirit through miracles. His knowledge of betrayal proved his psychic abilities. Jesus demonstrated life after death through his resurrection."

"I understand you, we share similar beliefs." he said.

"I firmly believe we only know parts of the truth. In the Bible there are stories of people being visited by angels. Through my experiences, I feel they were visited by their spirit guides. Angels are amongst us and come to our rescue. Spirit guides can actually communicate with us."

"I feel you're onto something here," he replied.

"Many people are experiencing spiritual activity. They are unsure of how to react, due to their religious upbringing.

141

People still fear persecution or going to hell."

"When I was a minister, many people attended weekly services. Going to church provided many with a sense of spiritual security for an afterlife in heaven.

"I feel the churches have damaged spiritual growth, by prohibiting spiritual experiences. The faiths are holding worshippers back from developing to their true spiritual potential. The faiths regurgitate the biblical stories. If people start communicating with spirits, it's considered sinful."

"How do you view mediums and spirituality?" he questioned.

"Mediums are extremely advanced souls with the ultimate spiritual connection."

Chapter Fourteen

DEALING WITH DARKNESS

Spirit had shown me a man in monochrome. He had squinted eyes, golden hair, and a leather jacket. The background was dark. A few weeks after joining an on-line dating service, a male matching the description approached me. Right away, I jumped to the conclusion that I was to date him.

Anything viewed in monochrome are lessons. Important events are revealed in color like a video. Anything repeated indicates the situation hasn't happened yet. Spirit kept showing the two golden heads together while dating Paul.

Before going to bed, I approached Mary Ellen with my situation.

"Mary Ellen, why do you keep showing me these golden heads? This doesn't make any sense. You already know I'm dating someone."

That evening I was awakened from a really enjoyable dream. I was shown a black and white video, which turned into color after a few seconds. It was of a wedding; the bride and groom were standing with their backs to me. The groom appeared to be a shorter thinner male.

"Why would you wake me up to watch a wedding? I don't like weddings. I'm glad it's not me."

The focus became the bride. I could see the side of her face. I took a double take. That bride was me. My unmistakable nose and my hair were revealed. The designer gown was absolutely beautiful. The dainty headpiece consisted of feathers and crystals. She weighed thirty pounds less than I did.

"Spirit, stop; I don't want this. I don't want to marry anyone ever again. Why would you shove a wedding in my face at three in the morning?"

Only the bride and minister leading the ceremony were completely visible. The bride appeared to be a little teary and overwhelmed, but happy at the same time. The groom remained hidden with dark shading, obviously a stranger. The floor had a rough texture to it. A small round signing table was in the corner near bare walls.

I lay awake trying to make sense of the scene.

"The groom I was shown was shorter than me. Paul is taller than me, which ruled him out."

The following night, Paul stayed over. While sleeping, I astral travelled. I found myself inside the Records Hall with Dan. On occasion, I spend time with my guides on the other side during my sleep. All the surroundings in the hall were white, clean and open. On the way back, I was running unbelievably fast down a long empty hallway. This sensation would be similar to being in a wind tunnel. Our spiritual bodies are very light and agile.

As I ran, Dan hollered, "Tell him you love him."

I was totally thrown off by the message. This didn't fit with my current life. Do I tell a past lover that I love him? I found this extremely confusing. Messages like this are extremely important, but not always meant for today.

My astral trip ended by the inside window of my office. Somehow I missed returning to my body on the way back. Foolishly, I attempted to walk through the walls without success. After becoming alert, I scrambled to my bedroom and reunited with my body. I woke immediately to find Paul awake and quite amused.

"You were out and ran into difficulties on your way back."

"How did you know?"

"I saw. Astral-travelling is something we share."

"It was quite the interesting trip."

"What happened?"

"Not much, except for something that my spirit guide said."

"What was said?"
"Don't take this personally. Dan said, 'Tell him you love him.' Paul we don't love each other. Love is kind, gentle and patient. We only like each other."

"What does this mean to you?"

"I don't know, but this message isn't about you."

Several days later, I woke in the night after hearing myself scream in agony. The pain was severe and relentless. After gradually crawling out of bed, I slowly made it down the stairs. My abdomen was in spasms, making it difficult to breathe or stand without holding onto something. This was ten times worse than active labor.

I eventually made it to my car, which was parked right outside my house. I drove in my pajamas. The pain was so horrific, I had to stop several times on the way to the hospital.

After arriving at the emergency, I parked the car. In the dark early morning hours, the parking lot was quiet; not a person was in sight. I got out of my car, locked the door and took a couple of steps; suddenly I was doubled over in pain. Breathing and moving had become difficult for a couple minutes.

"Spirit, help me."

The pain quickly subsided long enough for me to make it inside. I was immediately helped by emergency room staff and admitted to the hospital. I was on the verge of an abdominal rupture.

A doctor had come in to recheck things and started to lightly press on my stomach. My situation suddenly became worse. On morphine I found it hard to communicate. My mouth was dry and I was nauseated.

"How long have you been sick?" the doctor asked.

"I'm going to be sick," I moaned. "I need water."

"You can't have water, we might be operating soon."

My body started to quiver and heave.

"I want to go home," I started to cry.

"Nurse, sedate and comfort her. Let me know if she gets worse and we'll go into surgery right away."

I remember cool clothes on my head and neck before drifting off.

Hours later, I started waking up a little. I watched the soul of an elderly lady go to the light. A code alarm sounded shortly after. Staff ran down the hallway with a crash cart. The group stopped next door to resuscitate a patient. Another nurse came in to check on me.

"How are you doing, Laura?"

"I still feel very sick."

"Is there anything I can do for you?"

"No. The old lady's fine, I saw her leave."

"Laura, she's not fine. She's dead. We weren't able to save her. Do you need something for the pain?"

"No."

I drifted back to sleep and awakened to the sound of my cell phone.

"Is this Laura LaForce?"

"Speaking."

"This is Constable Rogers. I've been trying to reach you. I heard you have some information on the murder of Gerald LeBlanc."

"Yes ,Officer."

"Is it possible for us to meet today and go over the details?"

"I'm laid up in the hospital. Can you come here?"

"Seeing how you're not well, let's do this over the phone."
"Okay."

"Tell me what you know about Gerald."

"I worked with Gerald, eighteen months before his cold-blooded murder. He introduced me to Mike, a salesperson from their head office. Standing across from this man I immediately felt terrified. His energy was dark and evil, even though he was clean cut. I was shown Mike holding a pistol behind a head."

"Were you there when Gerald was killed?"

"No, I was shown through a premonition."

"Did you ever tell Gerald?"

"No, I knew he wouldn't believe me."

"Anything else you need to tell me?"

"Gerald appeared to me hours after dying asking me to turn in Mike."

"Do you know Mike's last name?"

"Trent."

"How old was he?"

"Early fifties."

"Can you describe him?"

"Mike had grayish blonde curly hair with sideburns, blue eyes, and a heavy moustache."

"How tall is Mike?"

"He is six feet."

"Do you know where Mike worked?"

"He worked out of their head office on the east coast."
"Did you tell anybody else?"

"Yes, a couple of other police officers."

"What ended up happening?"

"I was told that I was mourning, and not to worry, because they already had their man."

"Did you tell anybody else?"

"Yes, I ended up calling Sharon at Crime Stoppers."

"Do you have the file number?"

"Yes, at home."

"Will I be able to verify this?"

"Yes."

"Thanks for helping. Can I call you later if I have more questions?"

"Yes."

This all happened several years ago. On the evening news an accidental fatality at Bart's Industrial was announced. No names had been disclosed. Gerald's face appeared to me immediately.

The day before this happened, I had a strong urge to visit Gerald. He had been my boss. He was pleasant and nice, but visiting didn't make sense. I couldn't understand why, because I hadn't worked there in a long time. If I was to visit him, what would we talk about? I felt confused and decided to stay home.

Sometimes before people die, I have an overpowering urge to visit them. I dismissed the premonition a long time ago and carried on with my life.

Gerald appeared to me in a dream the night he died. He was lying in a coffin. He turned his head, opened his eyes and spoke in a raspy voice. "Tell them Mike did it." The next day a bullet hole was found at the back of his head by the medical examiner. How did the police miss a bullet hole in the back of a head on their initial visit?

Many people were affected by the situation. Gerald was a good loving person leaving behind a loving wife and children. Unfortunately, we have many flaws down here, which get in the way of serving justice. It will be dealt with on the other side.

I drifted back to sleep after speaking with the officer. Hours later I ended up in surgery. This is when everything became extremely familiar. Until now, I had forgotten about the vision last year involving an operating room.

The next day, the doctor came to see me.

"Your whole digestive track from top to bottom is extremely inflamed. I found three intestinal ulcers, one is abscessed. Biopsies were taken from each. I won't know more until the results come in. This will take about ten days. What I saw inside you is rare. This happens to people who are under extreme stress. Has anything stressful happened to you?"

"Yes, the past several years have been terrible."

"What happened?"

"Two years ago, I left my abusive husband, who tormented me for years. He became enraged. He and a friend had eleven strangers actively chase and torment me in groups of two, three or four. I feared for my life and still do."

"Did anything else happen?"

"I signed the house over to him, in hopes of safety. I pretty much lost most of my possessions, including my birth certificate. He fraudulently used my social insurance number. I was badly injured in a couple of car accidents. A close friend died and I lost a lover."

"Is there anything else you want to tell me?"

"No, it could cost me my life."

"What happens to you physically, when you're stressed?"
"I've ended up shaking, and coughing to the point of choking. My hair has fallen out in handfuls. I've experienced profuse vomiting and diarrhea. Sometimes my bowels and

bladder stop working. I have even broken a tooth during my sleep. The dentist discovered several of my molars had taken on the shape of toilet plungers. He mentioned it was due to clenching, but he had never seen anything this bad before."

"Does anything else happen when you're stressed?"

"I have woken up choking on vomit and unable to catch my breath. I've caught myself upon waking running in the middle of the hallway."

"Those are night terrors you're experiencing. I'm amazed you're alive."

By then I had tears in my eyes. The pain in my stomach had magnified. I hurt so bad, I could feel the heat of pain throughout my body.

"Do you want something for pain?" "Yes."

"I'll send a nurse in with something for the pain. We'll keep rotating antibiotics through the IV, until the infection and inflammation clears."

Paul showed up a couple times at the hospital, while I was recovering. The first time he dropped in with flowers and a big smile on his face.

"I'm glad to see you sitting up in bed. Are they sending you home soon?"

A couple of days later Paul showed up irritated.

"Do you want me to leave you alone until you get better? It's hard for me to see you this way. I worry about you dying. If you're going to die, I don't want to be here. Then he went on to explain why.

"You know when my old man was dying. I couldn't stand to

see him die. I told him good-bye and that I was leaving town. 'Are you sure you want to do that? You won't see me again, I'm not going to last another day. Son, this will be the last time you see me.' All I could say was good-bye Dad and I left crying."

Half asleep already, I said, "Don't worry about me. Let me sleep."

"When the doctor releases you, call me. I'll drive you home."

"Sounds like a plan."

Shortly after Paul left, my deceased friends Stephanie and Tony appeared beside the bed. Tony had recently died from heart failure. Stephanie had been gone several years. Her hair was curled and wavy similar to that of a sixties style. She appeared in a sweater and skirt with a veiled hat from the sixties. Physically she appeared fifteen years younger. Tony looked the same and he lip synced "Love you." He was a friend. We were never lovers, but there are many kinds of love.

The warmth and love on their faces made me feel at ease. Their presence provided me great comfort. Loved ones often show up near death or in times of need. Either they were here to take me home with them or to help me through this. I was okay either way.

Five years ago, I was arranging for a personal loan at the bank. Suddenly I saw Stephanie's face. I could smell and tasted the cold rotting scent of death and felt chilled to the bone. In the worse way, I wanted to run and scream. Instead, I sat with tears in my eyes. The thought of her dying was unbearable. She was like a mother to me.

"Spirit, please don't take her. I love her. I need her."

Three months later Stephanie had a heart attack, while out Christmas shopping. I was also out shopping at the same time, five hours away from her. While at the store, I briefly felt light headed and heavy pressure on my chest. I found a place to quietly rest until the sensation passed.

That evening, I received a call from Nelson, a mutual friend.
"Hi Laura, Stephanie had a heart attack this afternoon. They revived her, but nobody performed CPR in the first three minutes. She's on life support. Her brain has been damaged. We don't expect her to make it."

A couple of days later, the ventilator was removed. Stephanie remained unconscious, but continued to breathe for a couple of hours on her own. The minute before she died, she opened her eyes and smiled as she drew her last breath. I wasn't in the room when she passed. It was revealed through Spirit that Stephanie's father came for her.

Stephanie hung around for the first couple days after her death. She would set off her alarm clock at unusual hours. It crowed like a rooster! Flames on candles would flicker extremely high because of her energy. This all stopped happening after her funeral.

This was the first time I had physically seen her since she passed. When she was alive we shared many things together. Now she was here for me and so was Tony. After a few minutes they both vanished into thin air.

A couple of day's later things seemed to be improving. I was told that I could go home if I wanted to. Upon returning home I was 21 pounds lighter. Clothing hung off my body. My body was extremely weak and sore. Sitting and standing were difficult. Working was going to be out of the question for awhile.

Days later, I received a vision of my surgeon. He was clicking a ballpoint retractable pen against his lips, while reading the test results. This was followed by a white hand holding up white intestines, which meant healing.

Within the hour, I received a call from the surgeon's office to book an appointment. There was a long wait the following day to see him. He had been called out on emergency surgery. While sitting in a full waiting room, a man had become loud and annoying.

"I have the best job in the world. Would anybody like to guess what I do?" he said.
Everybody was silent.

"I'm a funeral director," he stated.

Some people were starting to shy away and became uneasy.
"Sir, we could work together," I offered.

"Are you a mortician?"

"No, I'm a medium. I could tell you what the dead want."

The guy's face turned beet red. He moved straight across the room and quietly took a seat. Giggling and laughter now filled the air.

An hour later, the doctor went over the biopsy results. Nothing was cancerous, but everything was extremely inflamed. I was prescribed a drug to deal with the inflammation.

Several weeks later, I was still feeling sick. I decided to call Henry a healer from a spiritual group I met with sometimes.

"Hi Henry, this is Laura calling."

"How are you doing?"

"I've been very ill lately and things are taking a while to clear up."

"I heard one of the other ladies talking about you."

"Is it possible for you to come out to my house in the near future? I need some assistance with healing."

"Yes, I'll come out this afternoon."

"Thanks, Henry."

Henry arrived a couple hours later. We chatted in the living room for a while.
"Laura let's get ready to start this healing session. Is it possible for you to sit on a chair, instead of lying on the sofa? It would be easier for me to work with you this way."

I gradually made it to an adjacent chair and took a seat.

"All I want you to do is close your eyes and relax," he said.

While Henry was assisting me with healing, I saw a field with hundreds of windmill like devices turning. After he finished working with me, I thanked him.

Weeks before falling ill, I felt a strong urge to secure disability insurance. After inquiring about the insurance, I found it too costly. Now I had no funds due to becoming severely ill. Had I listened, I would have had better financial control. Things went from bad to worse on a financial level.

By month's end I was broke and called social services for assistance, only find out I was $30 over their limit to qualify. They offered to help with prescription drugs. The food bank delivered food. A couple friends gave me money for rent.

"Laura you give so much to others. Let others give to you," reasoned Kate.

This part was hard on me. Prior to falling ill, I was self employed, the bread winner. To depend on other people was extremely difficult for me, but I was thankful at the same time for their generosity.

Two months later, I was driving to a gathering with friends. This was my first outing since I'd been sick. The following day, I was booked for an open house. I would be providing readings for business people. I had nothing appropriate to wear, because all my clothes were too big. I decided to wear a sweater and skirt, which would require the use of strategically placed safety pins to keep them from falling off.

Seconds later, I received a vision of a lovely brand new designer blouse and a floral skirt displayed on hangers, as I drove down the road. "Spirit, get real. Stop with the charades. It's bad enough, that I have nothing to wear. This isn't funny, I'm broke and I have no way of buying something like that," I complained.

I spent the evening with friends that I hadn't seen in a while. I started getting ready to leave, when my friend Cindy stopped me.

"Laura, I have something for you. Please come with me," Cindy grabbed my arm, led me to her guest room, and opened the closet door revealing the lovely outfit, which I was shown in a vision.

"When I was in California, Spirit told me to buy this for you."

"Thank you Cindy, it's beautiful. You'd never believe what happened to me on the way here tonight. I was shown this outfit on hangers, as I drove down the road. This is amazing. I was worried about having nothing to wear tomorrow. Thank you very much, I really appreciated it," I could feel tears welling in my eyes, as I gave Cindy a huge hug.

After arriving home, I called Paul to share the good news.

"Come over right after the open house tomorrow and we'll have supper together."

"See you tomorrow."

Spirit had sent me several visions warning me about him. Paul's outbursts were revealed as physical temper tantrums of a young child. I minimized the information received about Paul being hyper. In another vision, Paul was in front of a shattered stained glass window, kicking his feet while jumping through the air. Paul excelled in martial arts. One night I was repeatedly shown Paul kicking things. He seemed out of control. Paul must have anger issues, but I hadn't personally witnessed any of this.

While visiting at Paul's, he was heading outside to do a couple of things before dark. I started chopping a small onion on a plate. Paul noticed this on the way out the door. He flew into the kitchen screaming at the top of his lungs. After calming down he apologized for screaming at me.

"Please use a chopping board with my good knives, I don't want them ruined."

I was reheating yams in a frying pan. A tiny corner of a yam became darkened. The scorch mark was no bigger than a raisin. While ranting and raving, Paul ran up the stairs into the kitchen, jumped up, and kicked lower cabinet doors right beside me. He just missed my legs. The door was left hanging off its hinge. He grabbed the frying pan off the stove and scraped everything into the garbage.

"How could you be such a stupid bitch," he screamed.

"You ruined my fucking supper," he raved.

My heart raced in terror. Immediately my stomach started to cramp and grumble.

"Excuse me," I blurted as I ran to the bathroom. Anxiety

157

had taken its nasty toll. "Spirit, watch over me," I begged as I sat in misery on the toilet. Unfortunately, the bathroom door didn't lock.

"Are you okay?" he inquired.

"Please leave me alone," I begged. It took a while for me to calm down. I managed to join him for coffee later.

"I'm sorry Laura. I didn't mean to scare you. My Dad used to beat me if the meal wasn't perfect," he claimed.

"I accept your apology, please don't let it happen again," I responded.

"Laura, I've had a disturbing vision lately. You are with a darker haired man. The two of you are extremely happy together. I always thought you were the one for me. Now I only hope to have you in my future. I've always wanted a wife to care for me. I'm tired of being alone and I want to settle down."

"Paul, things would have to change. I don't feel safe around you when you're angry."
"I can change."

"Leopards seldom change their spots," whispered Dan.

Lately, I had also received numerous colored visions of a shorter dark haired man. He was in my kitchen, hugging me at the door and we were walking hand in hand. We seemed to be very happy and content together. I thought my imagination was running wild. This was something I wasn't willing to share with Paul.

The next day on a shopping trip Paul started yelling at strangers. He was particularly upset with a girl sending him to the cashier to pay for a purchase. It was Christmas and a very busy time of the year in any store.

"What is wrong with you, girl? Don't you care about serving the customers? Isn't that your job?" he questioned.

I was deeply ashamed of his actions, but didn't dare say a word. More than embarrassed, I was petrified.

Later that night, Paul called while I was in the shower. Upon arriving at my place, he was deeply aggravated.

"If you would have only answered your stupid phone, I wouldn't have had time to beat up those stupid assholes. I beat up two guys – threw one of the guys through a closed window. Hopefully I didn't kill the bloody bastard. If I end up in jail, it'll be your fault," shouted Paul.

"Why Paul?" I responded as my stomach turned.

"Stupid women should learn to answer their fucking phones."

"Why is that, Paul?"

"If stupid women would learn to shut up, there would be no need for women's shelters."

"Why did you beat them up?"

"They were lying about something. I went over to straighten things out. I hate liars. My old man was a lying piece of shit."

Paul raced to the washroom. I never knew how to interpret the visions Spirit had shown of him frantically turning on the tap and splashing water on his face. After witnessing this cold water habit, I assumed he did it to calm down. Perhaps this was some sort of OCD ritual. Paul lived with his abusive alcoholic father after his mother abandoned them. Paul was only eight when she left.

"Laura, I spent time in jail for beating the crap out of my old man. Put him in the hospital. The courts wanted to keep me behind bars. Those bastard cops hated me. After I was released from jail, I moved far away. I never want to see bars again," Paul said.

Alarmed with his story and witnessing his tantrums, old memories came flooding back to me. I gathered my courage and said to him,

"I remember being only four, when I woke up to find my condemned home empty. There was blood splashed across my parent's frayed white bedspread, splashed on the lampshade, spots all over the grey tiled floor. A while later a social worker showed up. At six, my mother held my head under water to punish me. Again at fourteen, she choked me to the point of everything turning black. Paul, we have choices with how we live our lives. I don't want to be afraid like this again."

For the past several weeks, a naked ghost of a well-endowed male had approached me.

"Excuse me," he would whisper, as he raced in front of me. The ghost would get down on one knee, clasping his hands together, as if to plead. He would then glare at me with a look of desperation.

Paul would often bitterly comment about his father's anatomy. He would often say,

"Laura, my Dad was a luckier man than me," said Paul.

"Why is that?"

"My father's cock reached the middle of his thigh. If I had a cock like his, I could have any woman I wanted. My life would be better."

"Can I see a picture of your father?"
Paul pulled the picture of his father out of his wallet.

"This is the only picture I have left. I destroyed the other family photos. Looking at him brings back bad memories."

Paul's fathers' photo matched the ghost. I thought he wanted me to help his son. Now I understood his genuine concern for my safety. His father was begging me to leave him.

It was late: Paul insisted on staying the night. Shortly after climbing into bed, he fell asleep. After being so upset, I was unable to sleep. In desperation, I called on Dan. I was overcome by feelings of apprehension and fear.

Finally I understood what spirit was trying to show me about Paul.

"Dan should I work on this relationship or move on? Show me who I'm meant to be with. I'm begging you. Please."

Right away, I was shown the silhouettes of two gold heads touching at the forehead. Dan had shown me this image regularly for almost a year. This seemed to be a very significant relationship. This information was just not sufficient. Seconds later I became deeply aggravated. Through frustration I became impatient and demanding.

"Dan, two gold heads doesn't give me enough, I need details. If this BS is all you have to offer, I won't be talking to you anymore. This includes anybody else up there. You'll have to find someone else to work through."

There was dead silence. No visions, no words, nothing.

Minutes later a vision took over the sight in my left eye. A stunning gentleman wearing a tuxedo was brought into focus. The top three buttons on his shirt were undone, disclosing the hair on his chest. The belt on the tuxedo was undone, almost touching the floor. It was as if he was standing right in front of me. He was so close I could have touched him. I sat speechless as I viewed him. His warm brown eyes were very inviting. Stylish wavy brown hair almost hid his receding hairline. His smile was warm and genuine. The unique shape of his nose was shown from different angles. A fresh growth of five o'clock shadow was present.

The mysterious man was surrounded by soft yellow light. He appeared to be thinner and shorter than me. At first he was smiling with his hands gently clasped together at this waist. Next he had a mischievous look on this face with one eyebrow raised, while making a silly gesture of escaping. This ushered into a look of total peace and calm. He had seemed aware of being watched for he was putting on quite a show.

What a relief! The threatening male sleeping beside me would no longer be part of my life. Paul was a lesson I would never repeat.

On the surface Paul could be charming and pleasant, yet his energy was dark and heavy. His negativity was overpowering and not only directed towards me. Paul was starting to reveal his true colors. We had only been dating for six months.

Thankfully we were not living together. Unfortunately we had recently exchanged keys. I feared him and I knew that, for me, the relationship was over. While visiting his place a couple of days later, I purposely left his key behind.

On my way out Paul was working on his vehicle in his yard. While backing out of the driveway he motioned me to stop. My car was in reverse, I had my foot on the brake. I unrolled my window.

"Where are you going?" he demanded.

"To town." He called me ten minutes later on my cell.

"How long are you going to be?"

"Paul, I won't be back. Your key is on your kitchen table."

"You're abandoning me just like my folks. You're leaving me on New Years Day!" he cried.

"Good bye."

I realized he had severe control and abandonment issues. He was angry, the month prior to my first radio show.

"Don't go on that radio show Laura," he snapped. If you do, you'll never be mine. You'll belong to all of them. Our lives will never be the same. Call the radio station and cancel the show."

"Paul, I already said yes. This is my decision, my calling. Please stop reacting this way. This is totally uncalled for."

While having New Year's supper with friends. I received a call on my cell phone from my residence.

"Where are you? I thought you were home and had hidden your car down the block."

"I am out."

"I am in your house waiting. I brought you supper."

"Enjoy it without me, Paul."

Thoughts of fear raced through my head. I needed this to end without hostility. Calling the police doesn't guarantee safety and could easily escalate the situation. Before heading home, I asked my friend Kate to call me throughout the evening. I instructed her to call the police if I failed to answer her call.

I had experienced other forms of stalking with Paul. He was also a medium, but drew on dark energy. I received a call while driving my car,

"Hi Laura, you should have gone right at that last 'T' intersection."

"How could you be so certain, Paul?"

"You just passed the Gateway turnoff. Turn left at the next set of lights and back track two blocks."

The phone disconnected. While driving in traffic, my cell phone rang again.

"Are you ever stupid! You missed the fucking turn. Better hurry, if you're going to arrive today."

A couple of days later I experienced anxiety while out. I had chauffeured my friend Holly to a 3 P.M. doctor's appointment. While sitting in the waiting room, a young lady on crutches arrived, taking a seat across from me. I saw images of her dying.
"Dan, what do you want me to do with this information?" I asked.

There was no reply. I felt badly for her. I didn't know how to handle this awkward situation. This young woman had an illness. I wonder if she knew her time was limited. The situation was out of my control. Within seconds, I could see the outline of Paul's astral body appear across the room.

Later on my phone rang, "Hi, Laura. You were sure one unhappy girl at three o'clock today. I don't know what to do for you. You should tune things out," he stated.

After arriving home, Paul stayed the night. In the morning I went to the landlord as soon as Paul was out of sight. Within the hour the locks were changed. Paul called me from the road. I calmly let him know my locks had been changed.

"Laura do you think that is going to be enough to keep somebody out?" he responded.

"It better be," I replied.

"Laura, you would call the police if you were being bothered, wouldn't you?" asked Paul.

"Don't try anything, Paul. I would call the police," I replied.

"I'll never call you again, Laura." Paul abruptly hung up the phone.

Looking back on the first vision I received of Paul, the area surrounding him was black. I had assumed it was an evening setting.

This dark was the reflection of his negative energy from a black aura.

Why had I been in a relationship with Paul? Some relationships are to assist us in healing at different points in life. A couple can help each other heal, but within reason. Many people have found themselves enabling a partner. Out of fear of abandoning their partner, they become victimized.

Part of our job down here is to love and respect ourselves. When we put ourselves first, these scenarios are no longer present. We do have the power to make changes in the direction of our choice. When we're ready for a healthy relationship, it will happen.

I desired a decent loving partner to share my life with. I wrote a simple letter.

Dear Universe,

I am seeking a special man in my life.
I want one man worthy of sharing my love and life with.
I want a healthy, happy, respectful, loving relationship, to
be shared in ways we both understand and appreciate.

Laura

Chapter Fifteen

SEARCH FOR MISSING GOLD

For months after I was shown this mysterious gentleman, I hadn't seen a trace of him. I started doubting his existence. My spirit guides had never been wrong. Who was I to question them? Spirit knows who or what is meant to be in your life.

Then I started questioning the appearance of the man who had been revealed to me.

Is he really shorter than me? I didn't date shorter guys. Can I handle five o'clock shadow? I like clean-shaven men. Perhaps Dan was toying with me and this was a joke.

In the past, I have jumped to conclusions, failing to accurately decipher invaluable information. When in doubt, I've learned to ask again. Sometimes answers are received instantly. Other times the answer will randomly show up in daily life. My guides have been known to offer me other unrelated events.

I decided to start searching.

"Dan, please show me more about this dark haired guy?"

When dealing with spirit guides, they can be extremely humorous.

I was immediately shown thousands of books instead.

The books had white covers with crisp black writing, with only three words "Journey into Spirituality. One word was to be on each line of the cover. I believe plain white covers were used to convey the title to me.

These books were coming off an assembly line. Many were in open boxes, and more were sealed in the factory area.

Was I to write this book? Prior to this vision, I had planned on writing a book, but I wasn't ready yet.

I decided to join an online dating service. After meeting several people, no one was matching up with my 'mysterious gentleman.' I would meet them in person, just in case their pictures were off. I would kindly let them know right away they were not the one I had been shown.

One night I saw the name Scott written in black letters, with a grey background in midair.

"Spirit, what about Scott? Is there something I should know?"

The following weekend a man by the name of Scott invited me out for supper. I cautiously accepted his invitation. While out for supper, we started to talk.

"Laura, do you really work as a psychic?"

"Yes."

"Are you a mind reader?"

"No, that's not how ability works."

"What can you tell me about myself?"

I closed my eyes for a brief minute.

"Laura, are you falling asleep?"

"No, but your wife is waiting at home for you."

I opened my eyes. Scott's face was scarlet red. He was

unable to make eye contact. He groped in his suit jacket in a panic, while he searched for his wallet.

"I'm sorry, I've got to go. I didn't realize what a psychic was capable of knowing. You're not a private detective, are you?"

"No, but your wife is already onto you."

By Mid-March I pretty much had given up on meeting others. The mysterious man in the vision hadn't materialized. I left my profile on-line and continued on with my life. I started planning a Cuban vacation with my friend Matt. We both needed a vacation. Matt had been assigned to me as a body guard through the Woman's Shelter. Months after retiring from my case, we became friends.

When booking the trip at the travel agency, we asked for two single beds. The people behind the desk weren't initially taking us seriously.

"Look, this isn't funny. We aren't a couple. To keep costs down we'll share a room, but we need our own beds," I piped up, and the snickering stopped.

"If you can't supply two beds, let us know. We'll bring duct tape to tape a line down the middle of the bed to establish boundaries," added Matt.

"How does two double beds suit you?" asked the travel agent, smirking. "Terrific." We booked the vacation and left the office.

Chapter Sixteen

SOUL MATES

Once in a while, soul mates meet. These are very deep satisfying relationships. They often copy each other and live linear lives. They are on the same wavelength the majority of the time. It is almost like they have known each other forever. Their connection is intense and the bond is strong. They share the same beliefs, values, tastes, and the way they show their love for one another. What pleases one usually pleases the other.

The communication is phenomenal. Each person looks out for their partner's best interests. Even while away from each other, they can tune in and feel what the other is feeling. During conflict, they go that extra mile to avoid hurting each other's feelings. They are compassionate and share a deep spiritual connection. These relationships are easy and extremely comfortable. These couples encourage the growth of each other's souls.

When faced with difficult issues, there is enough confidence to help see the situation through. They both end up stronger after facing the challenges as a team.

On a warm sunny March afternoon, I started reading my emails. I received the neatest letter ever from a gentleman. His approach was very friendly, down-to-earth, and genuine. His words reflected the nature of his soul. He had written this just for me. It wasn't one of those generic excuses many send out. This person had a very different air about him. He was only looking for a friend and, quite honestly, that's all I was seeking.

Dear Determined to Find,

My name is TJ, I'm looking for a special friend. A lovely

lady to capture life's precious moments with. Life is a spontaneous journey to be enjoyed. I noticed we share many common interests and values. I am the adventurous boy, who always wanted to know why I couldn't pet the tigers.

I've been told I look stunning in a tuxedo, but I'm comfortable in jeans. I know how to treat a lady, and the difference between right and wrong. A beautiful lady should be showered with affection and flowers. I'm searching for my soul's lost treasure. It would be nice to hear from you, if you desire.

Sincerely,
TJ

Dear TJ,

My name is Laura. I'm replying to your lovely letter. I do seek the friendship of a fine respectable loving man. I have many interests and can be extremely spontaneous. Life is full of adventure and meant to be enjoyed. I'm the type of girl who would open the tiger's cage and set him free. It was nice hearing from you. Write again if you wish.

Sincerely, Laura

While inspecting his photos, one stood out. He was standing at a distance near a filing cabinet. TJ's build and dark hair seemed to fit the vision. His other photos looked slightly off, because of his haircut and shade. Several days later we started to chat online.

A week later TJ asked for my phone number. Within minutes of sharing my number the phone rang.

"Hi, Laura. This is TJ calling," a gentleman's pleasant voice spoke.

"Hello TJ, it's nice to put a voice to your name," I had already heard his voice before; this was confirmation for me. Soon. I would somehow prompt TJ into saying thank you to make 100 percent certain.

"How was your day?" I asked.

"It was busy and hectic," TJ replied.

"And yours?"
"It was a fairly normal day," I replied.
"I understand you're into wildlife photography?" TJ said.

"Yes, I've enjoyed this hobby since childhood. I owned my first camera at nine, I answered.

"Same here," he claimed. "Do you have a favorite photo that you're particularly proud of?"

"I actually have two. One is of a black bear with his hair standing up on his neck. The other is of a wild goose protecting her nest of eggs."

"I understand you're a psychic medium. That must be an interesting career."

"Are you comfortable with me being a psychic medium?" I asked.

"I have no problem with that whatsoever; I find it interesting."

The conversation flowed. TJ was very easy to speak with. The energy on the phone was tremendous. At the end of our pleasant conversation, I almost blurted, "I love you." I immediately stopped myself.

"He is a stranger," I told myself.

"You don't know him, and you can't possibly love him.

What is wrong with you girl?' This took me by surprise. The words almost fell out of my mouth.

After hanging up, I immediately called my friend Matt, my old bodyguard, who had become a good friend. We were both preoccupied with the dating world.

"Hi Matt, how's the dating scene going?"

"Not too shabby. What about you?"

"I finally spoke with this neat guy TJ. The one I've been chatting with online. He seems like a really nice guy. At the end of our first telephone conversation "I love you" almost slid out of my mouth. Thankfully I was able to stop myself."
"Laura, that's too funny. You're usually in good control of yourself. How did that happen?"

"I really don't know. Can you imagine how inappropriate and uncomfortable that would have been?"

"He would have either run like hell or been highly amused," Matt laughed.

"Have you started packing for our holiday?"

"No, I'll start tomorrow. You know I expect to meet this guy. I'll always be your bodyguard, even though you're no longer a protected client."

"I understand."

"If you decide to meet up with him, let me know."

"Okay."

About a week later, TJ and I, decided to meet in person at a coffee shop. Upon entering the coffee shop my energy suddenly shifted. TJ was standing near the counter and started making his way toward me. The whole area surrounding him took on a golden glow. This moment was so powerful I felt like running. The energy of his soul was astonishingly beautiful and gentle. It wasn't love at first sight. I take a while to warm up to others.

We grabbed our coffees and found a place to sit.

"It's a pleasure to finally meet you, Laura."

"It's nice to finally meet you, TJ."

"Laura, are you analyzing me?"

"No, TJ, why would I do that?" I replied giggling.

I had an urge to match him up with the visions that I had been shown.

The color of his hair threw me off just a little.

"TJ, isn't your hair originally a dark brown?"

"Yes, I dyed my hair a couple of days ago to hide the grey. I choose to go a shade lighter," he replied while blushing.

TJ kept asking me if I was analyzing or scanning him. I kind of giggled and told him I wasn't. I didn't see it that way. I just needed to look at him from different angles. When I receive a vision I only have thirty seconds to view the contents.

TJ's hair from the front view and side view were a match to my visions, especially the way his locks of waves fell. The way his eyebrows danced over his eyes when he expressed himself too were identical. The shape of his nose, jaw line and the five o'clock shadow were all present and accounted for. The skin tone on the top of his hands was the same. The eye glasses were never shown.

I needed to absolutely verify this was him, through voice

and word identification.

"What would you say if someone held open a door for you?"

TJ smiled at me briefly, then humored me by answering.

"Thank you."

His answer, voice, and tone were identical to the reply I had heard three years earlier, after a client remarked about his wife's ability.

We grabbed another coffee and continued to talk.

We discovered that both of us had spent our younger years in the same neighborhood three blocks apart. We had played at the same park and attended the same church. He was a cub and I was a brownie.

Last year, we both moved at about the same time and literally traded places. He used to walk through my complex when it was being built. He only lived three blocks away, wondering what these places would be like. I lived in his county and I used to walk around the lake in his village, contemplating what it would be like to live there.

We had been unknowingly following each other for years, but had never met.

"Would you like to see a movie with me tonight? There's a comedy showing at the cinema."

"That would be nice."

While watching the movie, I could feel TJ's hand gently hold my hand. At the end of the evening, it was time to go home.

"Do you have any plans for supper tomorrow?"

"Besides eating, I have no plans."

"Could I pick you up and take you to dinner?"

"Yes, I'd be glad to join you for dinner."

"Is 5 p.m. tomorrow fine?"

"Yes, but I can't stay out late. I'm leaving for Cuba the following day."

"You're going to Cuba?"

"Yes, I'm flying out to Varadero."

"Are you travelling with friends?"

"Yes, I'm going with my friend Matt. He used to be my old body guard."

"Oh, that's different. How long will you be away for?"

"A week."

"You must really enjoy travelling."

"Yes."
"Can I walk you to your car?"

"Sure."

"Is it okay to kiss you on the first date?"

"No, it's never a great idea to kiss on the first date," I told him.

TJ was extremely decent. I had never dated a polite gentleman like him. It would have been okay to kiss, but I was testing him looking for his reaction.

The following evening TJ arrived on time, with a

bouquet of beautiful flowers. We headed out to dinner. This was when we discovered our similarities. We both ordered the identical things from the menu.

"Can I order the two of you something to drink?" asked the waitress.

"I'll have an ice tea," TJ ordered.

"Make that two ice teas."

"It's okay to have something else. You don't have to order the same thing that I'm having," mentioned TJ.

"This is what I usually order to drink when I'm out."

"Me too," said TJ.

"Are there any foods you're allergic to or dislike? I'm allergic to nuts, and iceberg lettuce, and I hate grapefruit."

"You've got to be kidding! Mine are the same."

"No, I started first," I said.

We continued to talk over supper. We talked easily, enjoying the sound of each other's voices. He told me about one of his visions.

"I had this weird experience a couple of years ago, when my mother died. The night before her funeral, she appeared to me dressed in a blue outfit. "Tell your wife you love her every day. Love your children." Then she disappeared.

"The following day at her funeral, my mother was dressed in the same clothes."

"TJ, you're a medium. I've experienced these kinds of things myself since childhood."

"My mother was like this, but I never really thought about it."

After driving me home, I invited TJ in for tea. I walked TJ to the door as he was getting ready to leave.

"Laura, would a goodbye kiss be okay with you?"

"Yes, a kiss would be fine."

After kissing his gentle lips in his warm embrace, our foreheads touched. Our third eyes connected. After this moment TJ really started to awaken on a spiritual level. He had had experiences in the past, but had dismissed them. Now he understood what this was all about.

TJ was the man presented to me the week before my first wedding. After fourteen years, and many visions later, we finally met.

TJ had always seen himself with a faceless long haired brunette female. He had spotted her while awake and in dreams. He went through this for almost twenty years. These visions disappeared for both of us after we started dating.

There was an unusually strong connection between us from the moment we met., sharing the likeness of twins. We found ourselves constantly copying each other. While driving down the road we moved our sun visors in the exact direction at the same time. We blurted out at identical words and phrases at the same time.

"Let's pick up some rice milk and stop for a London Fog at the Coffee Stop," TJ said as we were out for a drive.

"You took the words out of my mouth TJ. I was just going to say the same thing," I replied.

One night while talking on the phone with TJ, we started casually discussing our day.

"Too bad you weren't here, you missed a good supper. I made one of my favorites: pork chops with mushroom sauce and mashed potatoes," I teased TJ.

"I hate to burst your bubble, but I had the same. Too bad you weren't here, you wouldn't have had to cook it alone. This has been a favorite of mine since I was a young boy. Seeing how I'm six years older, you must have copied."

TJ and I have been known to shop for groceries and purchase the same items the on same day.

While TJ was on a business trip out of town, I started reading a magazine article on "How to Amaze Your Man." While studying the contents at home in Alberta, TJ was in the middle of an executive meeting in Nova Scotia. I was expecting a call from TJ later that evening after his flight arrived at the Airport. A couple of friends were visiting when the phone rang.

"Hi Laura, I'm back."

"Would you like to come over for tea before heading home?"

"Sure, I'll be there within the hour."

I didn't tell him I had friends visiting. I wanted to surprise him with a nice evening.

TJ's car pulled up in the driveway. Upon coming through the door, he shook his finger at me in a naughty manner with a smile on his face.

"What a naughty thing to do. You were being a bad girl earlier today," TJ exclaimed in a loud excited voice.

I must have looked puzzled. I had no idea what he was talking about.

TJ went on to explain what happened to him at the big business meeting. He ended up having to excuse himself from the meeting. Our company heard the entire conversation from the living room. They were quite impressed, and I was a little embarrassed. I never considered the effect studying this sort of material would have on TJ.

IMPRINTED MESSAGES

TJ stayed that evening. An entity was lurking in my upstairs hallway. TJ and I questioned the entity together for the first time.

"Is someone here? Show me a yes or a no," I asked.

My electronic calculator could be heard, from the office, as if it was adding numbers.

"Is there something you're trying to tell me? Press once for yes and twice for no," TJ said.

Again the calculator went off with a single hit.

"Is there something I can help you with?" I said. The calculator went off twice.

This scenario went on for about five minutes. I rushed into the office afterwards to examine the roll. I discovered it had been used. The numerical calculator had alphabetical imprints on the tape roll. My calculator is always turned off, when not in use. This is something I have not been able to duplicate.

On occasion, I have discovered other random alphabetical coded messages on this calculator's tape.

Another time I awoke at 4 a.m., by this calculator going off. I found this disturbingly eerie. I prefer to be visited while awake or approached while dreaming. All batteries have since been removed.

One night, my television had been plastered with messages from Spirit. I was joking with TJ, as I dusted the drawings off.

"Laura, do you think that's going to stop Spirit?"

"They can't draw on a clean screen."

"I bet they'll find another writing pad."

"You're probably right."
The following morning, I noticed a drawing on my living room wall above my couch. There was a drawing of the Roman numeral II, which kept changing from a numeral to a box. It seemed like a guideline, regarding the completion of this book.

As I work on the book, the details of the drawing constantly change. Presently, the outside of the box is solid and the interior is shaded half way up. Once in a while, the letter "S" is displayed in the box. The appearance is similar to the way grease shows through a paper bag.

I attempted to remove the drawing, only to realize it wasn't removable.

"Spirit I have heard of writing on the wall, but this isn't funny." I exclaimed. "I'm moving next month."

It felt awkward leaving this progressive drawing behind. I didn't know how I was going to explain this to my landlord.

The day for my landlord to inspect my suite had arrived.

"Spirit, please help me get through this inspection."

I had messages from Spirit on the living room walls. A lower hallway wall and baseboard were damaged from an enraged ghost throwing a large framed picture off the wall.

"Laura, your place is immaculate," the landlord said.

"There will be no extra cleaning required."

"Thank you," I replied.

"I don't know what's wrong with your living room wall. The paint must be defective. We'll be painting your place before the next tenants arrive."

The light suddenly went out, as we headed toward the hallway with the damaged wall. After she passed the spot, I flicked the lights back on.

"Laura, how has the site manager been during your stay?" she inquired.

"If something needs to be repaired, it generally doesn't happen."

The hall light started to flicker, while we were speaking.

"Does this happen often with the light?"

"Yes."

"I'll put in an order for an electrician."

"There's nothing wrong, Spirit is present and was agreeing with our conversation. I'm a medium and this happens all the time."

The poor lady turned pale, as if she had seen a ghost, and immediately opened the door letting herself out.

Chapter Seventeen

WHIRLWIND OF EVENTS

The Psychic Fair

Negative thoughts raced through my mind about the psychic fair TJ and I were heading too. We arrived in a huge city, in the middle of construction. The city map in the car was missing a couple of major streets to our destination. TJ learned I couldn't read a map.

"Which way should I be turning next?" asked TJ.

"Let's try going south." I had the map open, but I was frustrated and no longer attempted to figure it out.

"This isn't right. You're not even trying to read that map. You gave up blocks ago."

"Why don't we switch places? I'll drive and you direct."

"No way, not in this crazy city."

We arrived three hours late and management had given my booth away. My new location ended up being beside a psychic who dressed like a stripper. She'd flaunt her partially clad body by sprawling across the fluffy pink rug that covered her table top. I spent the remaining two hours, watching men circling her table and women racing away. I sat in my booth until the end of the day without a single reading.

Later that evening, we checked into our pre-booked motel room. The place ended up being a disgusting dive. Our nerves were right on edge, with being able to sense each other's energy, neither of us had seen each other this way before.

TJ came up to me and put his arms around me. "Laura, I

love you," he said.

With all the stress, I had shut down after a moment of silence.

"Laura, don't you love me?" TJ asked.

I walked away for a moment, to collect my feelings. I was feeling all sorts of things. I wasn't in a very loving mood. I suddenly recalled Dan's booming voice, as I ran down the Records Hall on the other side.

"Tell him that you love him." This is what Dan was talking about. I went back to TJ and gave him a huge hug.

"TJ, I love you."

In the morning, I was still feeling sorry for myself. In the bathroom, I encountered the residential ghost. The female entity was squatting in the corner of the floor looking destitute. Before I could say anything, she vanished.

This was a difficult morning. TJ and I were both miserable. The looming negativity was unsettling.

"Dan, where is this relationship was going?"

I was shown, a ring in a box with a huge rectangular shaped gem with rounded corners. It took up the whole vision.

"TJ, I hope you're not going to be offended. I'm going to wear an excessively low cut top today. The stripper in the adjoining booth won't stand a chance."

"I'm impressed. That's actually a turn-on." At the fair, TJ disappeared for a while.

When he came back he said "This is for you, my dear." He said it with a smile while handing me a tiny gift bag.

Inside was a beautiful necklace with matching earrings. The

purple stones were heart shaped.

"Thank you TJ, how sweet of you. Dan showed me jewelry earlier this morning."

"He sure knows how to spoil a surprise."

One of my clients dropped by the booth at the fair to share what she heard.

"Laura, watch your back. Madame Bertha is angry and is looking for the psychic who took over her area."

"There are no territories" I replied. "I was hired on by the shop in your town, after she refused to work the entire summer."

"Bertha approached me this morning wanting to know if I had seen the new psychic in town. I denied knowing anything. Before I could get away from her, she uttered a threat, 'When I find out who's working in my territory, there will be hell to pay.' Be careful, Bertha practices black magic."

Later in the day, I noticed Bertha from a distance, but she never approached me. After the event ended, we headed for home. TJ and I were out on the highway, when the wrath of Bertha struck. Suddenly, we found ourselves under psychic attack. We were both suffering from severe chest pain making it difficult to breathe. I started praying for help.

We decided to stop in the next town for a break. We kept ourselves calm and managed to ground ourselves. Together, we returned the energy back to the sender with love.

The following week, I was reading at the shop where Bertha previously read. During the middle of a reading, the tightly shut door burst open. I could sense my client's apprehension.

"I don't dare look," my client started to panic.

"Everything's going to be okay. Another psychic is angry with me. This is a weak scare tactic and there's nothing to fear," I reassured her.

Next, my meditation CDs were disturbed on the tabletop in front of us. It was almost as if they were being shuffled. We waited for the activity to stop before continuing her reading.

While reading the next client, my soul cards were being disturbed. This was similar to a person flipping through files in a filing cabinet. I chose to ignore the activity and it stopped.

A couple of readings later I kept feeling pressure on my left hand on the ring finger. I felt this a couple of times. I figured TJ was shopping for a ring and trying to figure out the size.

The Candlelight Supper

We had been very busy traveling to different towns and we both finally had a free weekend. I mentioned to TJ it would be nice if we could have a quiet night together at his place with a candlelight dinner on Friday night.

I felt earlier in the day that a proposal was looming that weekend, but I kind of laughed it off.

The candlelight supper was fantastic and very relaxing. After supper, he was busy showing me rings he had purchased to resell, asking me my opinion of them. He kept insisting that I try them on. I knew he had a hidden agenda.

We moved to the living room where only candles and the fireplace lit the room. TJ was complaining of being extremely hot, which was unusual. He briefly excused himself from the room and suddenly reappeared. TJ hit the floor so fast, I wasn't sure if he had lost his balance.

TJ was now in front of me, down on one knee. "I have something I want you to see." He opened a small box and inside was a beautiful sparkling ring, with a large rectangular purple amethyst stone with rounded edges and 14 surrounding diamonds which formed a fleur-de-lis.

"Laura, will you marry me?"

"This is for real," I could hear Mary Ellen declaring.

With all the nervous energy and visions unfolding at once, I was stunned.

"Yes TJ, I will marry you."

Chapter Eighteen

HEALING AND MIRACLES

Many people receive healings through Spirit. Some healings may only provide pain relief. At other times healing comes in the form of a miracle. Sometimes one must die in order to heal.

I was invited out to a dance one evening with some friends. A vision appeared of someone lying face up on a dance floor. I could see the grey pants, white shirt and the curly brown hair.

The band playing that particular evening was geared toward older people. I would rather visit than dance. While visiting, I was overcome by an uncanny urge to dance. Friends of mine were headed to the dance floor. When I suddenly jumped out of my chair and interrupted them.

"Excuse me, Liz. Can I please have this dance with Alfred?" I urgently begged.

After exchanging a couple of odd glances, Liz spoke up.

"Alfred, would you dance this one with Laura?" Liz asked him.

Alfred grabbed my arm with a smirk on his face and led me to the dance floor.

The lady who was dancing beside us suddenly collapsed to the floor.

"Oh my God, no," I uttered, as I turned my back in fear. I didn't want to see any more. Something inside me urged me to turn around and help.

187

A couple of us were starting to administer first aid.
"She has no pulse," a man shouted.

"She's not breathing," a woman added.

The lady had been down less than ten seconds. We were
preparing to start CPR, when I noticed my friend Betty the
healer, out of the corner of my eye. She stood away from the
crowd and lifted her hands in prayer. A flash of light passed
through the top of her head, out her feet and into the top of the
lifeless lady's head. The woman was instantly revived;
without CPR.

I helped administer first aid. It was easier to assist her by being
able to sense her injuries on my body. After the ill lady was
rushed to the hospital, a couple of bystanders asked Betty to
leave.

One evening, I could no longer contain my curiosity and I
called Betty.

"Hi Betty, its Laura."

"What did you request, while praying for the dead woman?"

"Laura, it wasn't complicated. I asked Spirit, if time was
allowed, could this woman have her life back."

"Was that all?"

"Yes."

"Were you shown anything else?"

"Spirit revealed her husband tormenting her and causing
her grief hours before her heart stopped."

Weeks later, I saw the lady who had fallen ill at another
dance.

"Hello there, how are you feeling?" I asked pulling up chair beside the woman at the table, where she was sitting.

"Better."

"Did you see anything the night you died on the dance floor?'

"I was floating above everyone, watching the commotion. I saw you helping, and another lady praying with her hands held high in the air. Before I knew it, I was back in my body." We sat silently for a few moments.

"How did you know where I was hurt, without me telling you? I wasn't bleeding. Are you a doctor?"

"No, I'm empathic."

"What do you mean?"

"I have the ability to feel what others are experiencing on a physical or mental level."

"What else have you felt about other people?"

"I have felt tired or sad after entering a room full of people. I have experienced the heart attack of a close friend, and the labor pains of a stranger."

"How on earth did you feel the labor pains of a stranger?"

"While walking into watch a school concert, I received a vision of labor. Twenty minutes into the concert, I encountered a bout of labor pains. The man sitting beside me was surprised when his wife announced she was in labor. After experiencing a couple more of her contractions, I felt compelled to interfere. I ended up telling the mother-to-be that her painful contractions were less than three minutes apart. I told her that she needed to go to the hospital before it was too late. At first she was upset, because she wanted to hear her son sing, but halfway through the next song she left. I heard through the grapevine her second son was born forty five minutes later.

"What happened when your friend had a heart attack?" Brenda asked.

"I received a vision of my friend Jocelyn, suffering a heart attack many months before it occurred. I warned her of the impending situation. One day while out driving with a friend, I started experiencing sensations of a heart attack. These sensations went on for a couple hours, until I received a phone call informing me of my friend's heart attack."

The Angels

Elizabeth was my first client of the day. I could feel her pain, as she limped to her chair.

"A man is here and he's showing me an oxygen mask."

"That's my dad! Is he okay?" she inquired.

"He's showing me how you used to draw in the dirt together with a branch. He's just written the words "girl" and "Mr. Martin", Do they mean anything to you?"

Tears were welling in Elizabeth's eyes.

"I used to call him "Mr. Martin" and he called me "girl.""

"You used to rub your father's whiskers and joke about the roughness."

Martin was standing at Elizabeth's side for almost fifteen minutes.

"Extend your right hand, with your palm up," I instructed her.

"My hand is warm, it's almost like he's holding my hand." "He is holding your hand."

"I love you, Dad."

"I love you, girl," he said before vanishing.

"I never got to say good-bye to my father before he passed. He was unconscious when I arrived at the hospital and he never recovered."

"I can feel the pain in your foot, is it okay if I do some healing work on you?"

"Yes."

"Put your foot on my lap and we'll give it a try."

After briefly hesitating, she put her foot on my lap. I gently placed my hands on her foot. I closed my eyes. My viewing area turned pure white. I could see the sound waves. The healing mother arrived.

Only one side of her face is revealed, with her captivating white eye. The other half shaded.

"Mother, please help Elizabeth's foot." Suddenly, excessive energy flowed from my hands to her foot. I held her foot until the surge of healing energy stopped. I slowly opened my eyes and saw Elizabeth crying.

"How are you?"

"Thank you. I can't believe it, the pain's gone, for the first time in twenty-five years. I can put my foot on the ground without suffering." Elizabeth walked gracefully out the door and down the steps without a limp after her healing.

Immediately after she left, dozens of tiny golden singing angels appeared in front of me. While circling my table top, they sang in unison. This heavenly song resembled a high pitched chime or siren like sound.

I had just entered the No Fuss Aesthetics Salon for the first time to enquire about electrolysis. I needed more information on the available hair removal procedures. To ease my concerns, I needed to see the facility in person. A man lay silently on a lounger beside a wheelchair. I stood at the front counter for a few moments before breaking the silence.

"Excuse me, Sir, have you seen the person in charge?" I inquired. "I am," replied the man. "Somebody will be with you in a while. Have a seat," he snapped. I seated myself a distance from the man, feeling the negativity.

"Useless people," he audibly uttered under his breath. "What a waste of space!" My first impressions of Bob were anger and rage. Underneath all of those emotions was severe emotional and physical pain.

I drew a deep breath before asking, "Is something troubling you?"
"Yes, those useless bastards," he angrily replied. "The bastard that just walked by my window doesn't deserve those legs or his body."

"Why not?" I responded.

"He's a useless piece of shit," he retorted.
"Do you know him?" I asked.

"No of course not," he answered.

"I'm Laura, may I ask your name?"

"Bob," he replied.

"Bob, I feel uneasy in your facility with your negative attitude. It is important for me to feel secure in an unknown situation."

"Shirley, get your ass out here," Bob hollered.

Moments later, Shirley appeared from around the corner. After going over the details and seeing the spa, I booked a couple of appointments.

The next day, as I waited for my appointment, Bob was in a slightly better mood.

"Laura, what do you do?" Bob asked.

After a brief hesitation I told Bob, "I am a psychic medium." He was silent for a couple moments. "A fortune teller," he responded.

"No Bob, I have a gift of being able to help people with the assistance of the spirit world," I explained.

"What can you do for me? Do you know why I am in this wheelchair? Will I ever be free of pain? Do I die like this, Laura? " Bob wanted to know what I could do for him.

I realized he was in severe pain. I could feel it. I was very reluctant to do anything. Deep inside I knew if any healing was going to occur, the anger was going to have to be dealt with first.

"Bob your anger is extremely destructive to you in all aspects of your life."

Bob started yelling at me, "My anger is not the issue here." Tears were running down his face, he started sobbing loudly.

"Do you know how much I hurt all the time? I'm only forty years old. This just isn't fair! How much money would we be talking to heal me?"

"Bob, you are not ready, your anger is out of control. Please calm down," I replied.

We were sitting, looking out a store window into the street. He would be extremely upset at the sight of any male walking by.

He would angrily mumble, "This guy should be in my place instead."

I needed Bob to come to his senses. He needed to calm down before I could assist him.

"Why Bob?" I asked.

"He looks like a useless prick," he replied.

"Do you know him?" I asked Bob. Bob sat in silence. He didn't even answer.

I started pointing out he was being judgmental and angry
.
"Bob you don't even know these people. You are lashing out at them in anger and pain. Please correct me if I'm wrong."

Bob sat there silently with his head down, no longer making eye contact.

"Bob this is about you, not the strangers who walk by. You are in a spiritual rut. You can't even see it. Ranting and raving does not invite spiritual assistance of any kind. Bob I cannot do anything for you at the moment. You need to part with some of your anger. I have to go. I'll be back in a couple days. Allow yourself to take some time to search your soul."

Upon arriving home, I had placed several calls to Betty the healer. I felt that with her experience and expertise, she would be best to assist Bob. A couple days passed and no calls had been returned.

A couple of days later, on my next visit to the salon, Bob had calmed down. I could sense a huge shift in his energy. This was a great indicator of his willingness to listen.

"Bob I can see that you're in better spirits today. It seems you are ready for some healing."

Bob looked very anxious.

"Can you help me today, Laura?"

"Yes, Bob. Right now."

I started working with him immediately. He was wheelchair bound, with no feeling in his hands or arms. He was no longer able to physically feed himself. This was extremely hard on him.

Shortly after we started, the store's door buzzer rang. I noticed a couple of his friends came in. They quietly sat down in the waiting room watching the session. Healing Mother had surrounded him with her healing energies. I was shown to work the crown chakra and back of the neck. I was shown to pull negative energy out and replace it with positive energy. Just before finishing, I was shown with arrows where to send the positive energy. This energy boost went on for a couple minutes. As soon as Healing Mother's energies subsided, I stopped.

"Thank you, Mother, for helping Bob," were the first words out of my mouth.

Immediately after the healing session, Bob was in tears, but different tears. These were tears of joy.

"Oh, My God! Warmth is rushing through my arms," exclaimed Bob. "I can feel sensations in my hands, they are tingling," he stated before breaking into a loud sob. "I haven't felt my arms in a couple of years. I can't believe this, it is totally unreal," he claimed.

"Close your eyes and rest awhile Bob."

"I never expected this to work. What do I owe you, Laura?"

"Nothing, Bob. Continue to feel the goodness of Spirit and

give thanks to God," I said.

After finishing the healing session, I noticed that Bob's friends were no longer there. A couple of minutes later, some of Bob's friends returned to the room. The energy had been so strong they had to leave the room. I wasn't even aware they had left the room, while I was working. When I am assisting in this capacity all I see is Healing Mother and her instructions. My only concern at the time of healing is the soul in need and Spirit.

Later that evening, Betty finally returned my call. "I see you are doing what you should be doing. You have done well!"

"Thank you, Betty, but I really needed you earlier to help this guy. I have been trying to reach you for days."

"Laura you're ready to fly on your own. Spirit advised me to let you handle the situation with him. Otherwise you would have never assisted him or anyone else on your own," she claimed.

A couple of days later, I dropped by to check on Bob.

"How are things with you, Bob?"

"Great, I'm going to be better before summer."

"Bob your recovery is going to be gradual. I was shown by Spirit approximately two years, providing your stubborn attitude doesn't disturb your physically healing."

A month later I dropped by to visit Bob. I had just walked through the door of his salon.

"Laura I am glad to see you. I have something to show you."

Bob took a deep breath and used his arms to push himself out of the wheelchair and walk six feet unassisted.

"I am happy for you, Bob. This must feel great. Remember to

take things slow," I reminded him.

A week later I dropped by to visit Bob. He had overdone things and had regressed. He sat looking fairly despondent.

"Hi Bob, what's wrong?"

"I guess I overdid things. I really wanted my healthy self back. Do you know what it's like not to walk, Laura?"

"Yes, Bob, I've been there before," I responded.

In a shocked voice Bob replied "You have?"

"Yes, I was nineteen years old and had a severe muscle disorder. I lost mobility of my hips and legs. What put you in the wheelchair, Bob?"

"After several accidents and fights, my body just gradually stopped working. I have been confined to a wheelchair for the past two years. My girlfriend Shirley is a great lady and has taken good care of me.

Six months ago, my arms went numb and my hands lost all sensation. I could no longer feed myself, among other things. When things got bad I chose to have my hair shaved off.

Shirley has been a Godsend. She takes care of me around the clock."

After working on things again, he is slowly regaining his health and independence.

The Three C's

One evening, I received a vision of three "C's" on a man's chest. The following evening, my client Calvin had arrived requesting a healing session. TJ and I dimly lit the room with candles. We stood silently around Calvin, waiting for

Healing Mother to join us.

Minutes later, sound waves appeared. A very strong energy became prevalent. My line of vision turned pure white and was accompanied by black swirls.

A pair of white glowing hands became visible. Healing Mother lit up the area, where I was to put my hands. I pulled the negative energy and replenished it with positive energy, under Healing Mother's gentle guidance.

Calvin was pain free immediately after this session. My headache and back spasms, which I had had all day, were released during his healing.

Chapter Nineteen

DEATH AND DYING

Prior to death, many people have out-of-body experiences. Sometimes our loved ones make their rounds in familiar areas. Other times they briefly check out the other side. This usually occurs during relaxation or in a dream state, while the soul is preparing to go home.

Many loved ones receive visits from the other side on their death beds. Often, deceased relatives or close friends show up to comfort and invite them.

Sometimes before the soul leaves the body, warmth gushes through the solar plexus. This warmth radiates to other parts of the body. This happens seconds before leaving the body.

Then, a floating sensation sets in just before the soul lifts out. Death can be a very peaceful experience.

Greg

Greg was quite ill in the hospital recovering from a heart attack. One evening, I was babysitting a little girl at home. I was in the middle of helping her brush her teeth.

Suddenly an apparition of Greg appeared beside me in my peripheral line of vision. His skin and aura had a grayish tone. Greg came through with his full body partially materialized. Thirty seconds later he attempted to materialize again. Greg died the following day.

Martha

Martha was talking with family members, while lying on her death bed. Suddenly, her face lit up with excitement as she announced, "It's really nice to see everyone. Father is here and I'm going home with him." she stated. Martha drew her last breath and died the next moment.

Peter

Peter celebrated all occasions in life to the fullest, including his death. It was his daughter's birthday, and Peter insisted a cake was to be brought to the hospital. While singing "Happy Birthday," Peter went into cardiac arrest and died.

William

Tracy and William, were a married couple that I knew for years. One evening I felt an unusual urge to visit William. Tracy and I would get together once in a while, when he was at work. I was preoccupied with running my busy company. I decided to drop by another time. Three days later William suffered a heart attack and died hours later.

During his attack he was seeing children. "Why are children lined up here?" he asked.

This was seconds before losing consciousness. The soul is often aware of different surroundings before death actually occurs. William passed hours later.

Chapter Twenty

COMMUNICATIONS

Weeks later, Tracy called me, with excitement in her voice.

"Laura, can you come over right now? William's trying to talk to me through the television screen."

"I'll be over in five minutes."

After I arrived at Tracy's, the message was still visible. This resembled a worded transcription, which would usually be displayed under a show. Only the words, "God this is driving me crazy," were revealed across a blank TV screen.

Heavenly Couple Interacts

My client Brad excitedly sat down for a reading. He was one of the first clients to insist on pushing my limits.

"The dead know everything, right?"

"Yes."

"Well, let's call on my mother and father."

"I've always waited for the loved ones to show up. I've never actively invited them to attend. I don't even know if I'm comfortable disturbing them."

"Please do it for me. I need to talk to them."

We put our hands on the table top palms up and attempted to invite his family in.

"Spirit, could we please talk to Brad's mother and father?"

I quietly waited for a response. Two faces came in beside each other.

"Your parents have arrived together and they're happy to see you."

"Ask my parents if they're satisfied with the way the wills are being handled?"

"Your father is shaking his head no and a tear is on his right cheek. Your mother is giving him a stern look and shaking two fingers at him, like this." I went on to demonstrate this.

"That was exactly how she used to scold him. The tear on my father's cheek is actually a scar."

The Red Jelly Bean

A lady briefly hesitated before entering my booth at a fair. "I'm hoping you can give me what I've come for."

"I'll try. May I ask your name before we start?"

"Marsha."

Upon closing my eyes, I could see a small white orb. A couple of seconds later a young girl manifested.

"I have a young girl here wearing a white frilly dress, with big red gooey splotches on it. She is pursing a red jellybean between her lips and red goo is running down her chin."

"Oh my God, that's my Heidi. Is she okay?"

"She is smiling and giggling at you, she's skipping away,

while blowing kisses."

"I'm so happy Heidi showed up. Our family still reminisces about Heidi wearing her white frilly Easter dress, her mouth stuffed with red and white jellybeans. There was a red mess everywhere, including her lovely white dress."

"Is there anything else I can help you with?"

"My mother, a devout Catholic, passed several months ago. She recently appeared to me during a dream. While visiting, my mom mentioned 'If she knew in life, what she knows now, she wouldn't have spent so much time on religion.' I found this message confusing, because this goes against what I was taught."

"When you are ready, you will decide what is appropriate for you. Did I help you today?"

"Yes, thank you."

Double S

A lady came to see me for a reading.

"I need some answers to challenges in my life. I heard others talking of your extraordinary psychic abilities. I'm hoping you won't disappoint me."

"Can I have your name please?"

"Joan."

"Let's join hands and start your reading. Your mother is here, she's standing on your right. She's wearing a long pastel green dress and bright pink lipstick."

"That was my mom's favorite dress and shade of lipstick."

"A soul of a male has shown up in a blue orb. This soldier

203

is in his mid twenties, and has written a scripted "*SS*" in mid air." I drew what I had seen on a piece of paper for her.

Joan was ecstatic, "That's my brother Max. The "SS" is significant. This detail alone verified his place in the army. It was actually written that way."

Max saluted, pivoted and marched away.

"Thank you for seeing. Have a great day."

Red Heart

Beth came for a reading at a psychic fair I was attending.

"I'm low on funds and I desperately need to know if my son Anthony is okay."

The moment Beth sat at the table, Anthony was beside her.

"He is sending a letter "K", which means he's fine. He wants you to stop crying, and to stop feeling guilty. He's wiping his eyes with a tissue which is symbolic of this. His death wasn't your fault."
"Anthony, I love you."

"He loves you and has sent his love with a vision of a solid red heart."

"My shoulder is warm."

"He's touching you. Enjoy his loving energy."

"Thank you for helping me. This meant a lot. What do I owe you?"

"Nothing."

The Best

A family had come for a reading. This family recently lost their father and husband, Keith. He was already there without being invited. He kept spelling out THE BEST with a huge smile on his face. I really felt this was inappropriate. These folks were mourning.

"How is my father?" asked one of the sons.

"He's been spelling THE BEST out in mid air repeatedly." I finally replied.

There wasn't a dry eye in the room. I waited for everyone to pull themselves together.

"My father said THE BEST, seconds before he died. That's how he referred to us."

Keith vanished into thin air.

The Sisters

Theresa had just sat down for her reading, when a loved one kept trying to appear. The white orb kept showing up on the right hand side of Theresa. My client was apprehensive and shaking. She had never had a reading before. I decided to let, the loved one wait, until I was sure she could handle things. Halfway through I stopped the reading.

"Do you have anything you wanted to ask?"

"Yes, how is my sister, Monica? I was hoping she would show up."

"She's been here the whole time. I didn't want to scare you."

Monica had been showing me details of the accident which had killed her.

"Did she suffer?" Theresa asked.

"No."

"Your sister is flashing different shaded swatches of pink," l said.

"That was our favorite color."

"Monica keeps showing me a tiny silver tea pot, then shows me hands dipping into a ceramic teddy bear cookie jar."

Theresa's eyes welled up with tears.

"We used to have tea parties and raid the teddy bear cookie jar." Monica told Theresa she loved her and vanished.

The Boy

I was having coffee at a cleaning client's home. An apparition young boy appeared to me in the kitchen.

"Tell her, Hi Auntie Mommy," he quietly begged.

The boy went on to show me someone closing his eyes after his body was pulled from the water.

"You need to hold on," I told him through telepathy.

"There's a young boy beside you. He's about six years old with dark brown hair and brown eyes. He drowned and didn't have a chance to say goodbye," I told her.

Her face went a million shades of white, her shock was so severe. I thought she was going to pass out.

Minutes later, she responded to me; "My nephew Tom died last year on vacation."

Mildred

A client came for a reading. In less than two seconds after sitting down, a white orb appeared on her right side. The energy was very strong. I closed my eyes to focus on the orb.

"There's a woman beside you in her early 70's. She's decked out in hot pink, from head to foot. Her bottom teeth protrude, when she smiles. She keeps showing me the letter M."
My clients face beamed with great joy.

"That's Grandma Mildred. She just loved hot pink."

Louise

Right at the beginning of a reading, the outline of a woman appeared beside my client, Faith.

"Faith, your mother is here," I said. "Put your left hand over slightly above your right shoulder. Can you feel her energy?"

"Yes."

"Your mother keeps showing me a brightly lit kitchen with hanging pots and pans."

"My mother and I spent many hours in the kitchen together. She was in her kitchen from dawn to dusk and thoroughly enjoyed it."

"Your mom keeps showing me a single antique candlestick holder."

Faith's face lit up.

"That candlestick holder belonged to my mother's mother," she claimed.

After a while Louise started fading. She asked me to tell Faith that she loved her before vanishing.

The Aborted Soul

Liz came in for a reading. On her right forearm was a little white orb of an infant.

"Liz, you had an abortion several years ago. Your daughter's soul remains with you."

Liz immediately broke into tears.

"Is she okay? Tell her I'm sorry. I regret what I did. I've been severely depressed since the abortion 10 years ago. I thought the baby would go to heaven or be reincarnated to another life."

"Your baby will remain attached to you for the remainder of your life. Many see the unborn as soul-less, but this is not true. We choose our lives prior to conception, nothing is accidental or coincidental."

Chapter Twenty-one

SUICIDES

A blue orb appeared to me during Terri's reading.

"A young man is here to say hello. He's very sorry about the way he left you. He fell backwards on a concrete floor after shooting himself in the head."

"Oh my God, that's my brother Shawn," she cried. "Is he okay? Tell him I miss him."

"He can hear what you're saying," I told her.

"Is there anything else he wants to share?" she asked.

"He keeps showing a tiny bouquet of daisies, which were placed on his coffin."

"Twenty minutes before his funeral, I rushed out and picked some daisies for his casket."

"Your brother has been witnessing all the mourning and devastation his death caused. He wanted to end his unhappiness. He didn't realize the pain he would cause others."

"Tell Shawn I love him."

"He knows."

He sent her an image of a daisy in a heart and walked into the light.

The Overdose

A blue blob appeared to the right of an elderly lady during

one of my readings.

"Sheila there is a man standing beside you. He's a child of yours."

"That's my son Pierre. Is he okay?"

"He is blinking back the tears in his eyes and he's sorry he took the three bottles of pills."

"He was always blinking back his tears in life. Maybe this wouldn't have happened, if he had allowed himself to cry."

"He feels helpless watching you cry at night. He tries to comfort you, but you don't feel him."

"My shoulder's warm! Is he touching me?"

"Yes."

"He wants you to know he loves you."

"Pierre, I love you very much and always will," she stated.

"Did he make it over to the other side?"

"No, he's been earthbound since his death, but he's leaving for the other side." I told her. He's walked toward a lit doorway, before he stepped into the light and disappeared.

The moment I started a reading, a client, a disruptive negative ghost showed up. He literally stood between us, looking me in the eyes.

"I did it," he laughed. "I did it."

He was smiling, and was extremely pleased with himself and his actions. His displays were mischievous and out of sorts. He would go as far as to spell the words "I did it" out in midair.

The situation was upsetting. My distraught client wanted to know why her father had killed himself on her bed. Her spirit guide provided the answers she need for closure. Her Guide revealed that her father was insane. Dying on her bed was never part of the plan. Shortly after overdosing in the kitchen, her father became weak and dizzy. Her bedroom was the closest place to lie down.

Vera came in for a reading.

"My late husband David took his life several months ago. I need some closure," Vera explained.

We joined hands at the beginning of the reading. At first, I was surprised to see only Vera's spirit guide present to relay messages. I wondered where David was. Most suicides return to apologize.

"Your husband was an evil man. He beat you and molested your sons. David went out of his way to destroy others. This brought him gratification."

"David was a horrible man, I never loved him. He forced himself on me on our first date. That night I conceived our son. After David found out I was pregnant, he threatened to tell my mother, unless I married him immediately. If my mother had known we'd had premarital sex, she would have disowned me."

"Vera, Spirit has brought in David to witness the damage he has done. He is detained, restricted and encapsulated in a tiny charcoal colored orb, compressed to the size of a quarter. He is on your right about three feet away. He won't be able to hurt you or respond in anyway. Vera, let everything thing out, it's your turn. Tell him how much he's hurt you and the boys."

"David, you made my life a living hell. For many years I stood by you faithfully. You hurt me and the people I love. Eventually my life didn't matter. I felt like an ashamed slave. I started dying inside. I'm relieved you're dead." Vera broke

211

down sobbing. "Everyday I was with you, I wished you were dead. Everyday, I was at your mercy. Many times I wanted to leave, but I was scared you would kill me. My life's been ruined because of you and your violence, your drinking and your drugs. You were never fucking sober. I suffer from anxiety and depression because of you. I had dreams before I met you. David you ruined my life."

"Vera, David is no longer in the room. Spirit has taken him back."

"Why didn't they destroy that piece of shit?" she commented.

"I don't know the answer, Vera," I responded.

Chapter Twenty-two

GHOSTS

Ghosts are deceased souls with issues. A sudden or tragic death can cause a soul to linger in between for a short time. Unfinished business can keep a soul earthbound.

Ghosts do have choices, and continue to make decisions in the realm in which they exist. These ghosts have fears and beliefs which prevent them from crossing over.

Negative ghosts actively resist the light and cause disturbance, much like they did in life.

Many times victims of foul play have appeared to me as ghosts immediately after dying. Sometimes they show me what happened. At other times they display a visual image and initials of their killer. Occasionally they show the location of their remains.

GHOST STORIES

The following stories are vignettes of ghost stories.

Chad

I was out cleaning a house when my cell phone rang.

"I can't believe this." TJ exclaimed.

"A missing person's bulletin had arrived on his workplace email. I don't understand why this notice was sent here. This originates from eastern Canada."

Before TJ could go any further, a ghost of young male appeared to me in my client's hallway.

I saw a blonde haired boy of approximately twelve, trying to come through the hallway. I needed to get home to deal with him. This would deeply disturb my client.

I raced home and looked through my email to see the missing person's photo. The photo on the bulletin matched the ghost I saw at my client's. Chad had passed and was stuck in between. According to the bulletin he had been already missing a week. Chad kept reappearing, aimlessly around in a total loss. He was distressed and crying for his mother.

He kept showing that he was in a field of tall grass close to the tree line. The search party hadn't gone for enough and missed him.

Chad had spelled out the names Eric and Vic in midair. I assumed these were names of people. I was also shown a keyhole, which would represent a crescent cul-de-sac. After sharing this with TJ, he had a hunch the names were coordinates. Upon reviewing maps these coordinates were real. I knew nothing about that area of the country. We strongly feel the person responsible for Chad's death resides in this crescent. This would be approximately 90 minutes from where Chad's body was found.

Chad showed me he had been roughed up and asphyxiated. Some people play a dangerous game where they choke each other. This time it had turned deadly.

Communication had gone on between Chad and I for about five days. I was shown a white forensic tent the night before Chad was found.

Authorities ruled his death accidental, due to injuries. I was shown asphyxiation with upper body damage, which was not what the report claimed. Oddly enough, the people who found Chad mentioned that it seemed as if he had been recently placed there.

Nicole

Nicole's cold case was brought to my attention by Judy a client. I was asked if I could locate a woman who had disappeared many years ago. Suddenly, I had an apparition of heavier lady in front of me. Nicole's hair was up in unusual curls and she was dressed in a warm coat. A strange male had stopped by her house with a map looking for directions.

I was shown a small bridge and a pipe-like structure. She kept showing the number five for mileage. There was a definite struggle between the two. The stranger took an oval rock and hit the back of her head. This stranger was a white male late forties to mid fifties, with whitish blonde, brush cut, balding hair. He was approximately six feet, with broad shoulders and a strong muscular upper body. He placed her in a shallow grave and covered her remains with a fifty pound bag of a white powdered substance.

The only thing that threw me off in this case was Nicole went missing in the winter. The burial area seems to have the appearance of early spring. Taking the snow away gives a more defined location of her body. This is what I figure the scenario is in this case.

Another male is either indirectly involved or knowledgeable, in this murder. This male was about thirty eight years old. He had dark hair, a receding hairline, brown eyes, a heavy moustache and a round face.

I took a moment to put together what I had seen.

"I know this is going to sound odd, because this is a rural area. Nicole has shown me a little bridge and a pipe like structure under it." Upon mentioning the bridge my clients face lit up verifying the bridge. I brought up Nicole's unusual curls. Judy then disclosed that Nicole had disappeared in curlers."

Judy and I, decided to drive out to the site the next day. When we arrived at the bridge, I started to feel an extremely strong pull. My client drove a little further up the road wanting to show me the area.

"We need to turn the car around, and go back to the bridge, because we passed her. Nicole is pulling so strong on the back of my head that it hurts."

After turning around, the middle of my forehead (third eye) was pulling very strongly again.

Getting out of the car, I faced the direction of the pull. I then started moving forward with the pull. The forward pull ceased and thirty seconds later I felt the pulling again.. I stepped sideways once and the sensation stopped. Now all I had to do was recall what she had shown me.

She had shown me a series of three different fence posts. The different fence posts were one rebar, one metal and one wood. There was a major point of interest between the second and third post. Nicole was on the north side of the river, at the crest. Her body lay east to west and was approximately eight feet from the river bank.

Spirit took over, showing me she was only 31/2 to 4 feet down. I was shown two stick figures with the grave depth coming to the top of the thighs. I was shown that her part of her skull and the large bone from the shoulder to the elbow will be found. Her killer has since passed.

This information has been relayed to the police in the area. A year has passed with absolutely no action. I have heard through the grapevine the sergeant is leaving to another area. This old cold case is probably is of no interest to him. I understand it takes money to excavate and exhume a grave.

I returned to revisit the site with TJ, in the hope of finding Nicole.

"TJ, if we find Nicole's body, we might end up separated." I started.
"What do you mean separated, is there something about us you've seen?"

"No, if we find Nicole's body the police won't interview us together. She was killed when we were children. Tell them exactly what I've told you and we'll be all right."

It took us an hour to dig a hole two feet in diameter and almost four feet down. The water table was reached at approximately four feet. This matches the depth of the grave revealed by Spirit. We could feel Nicole's presence, but we were unable to locate her. If you miss a body by an inch, you'll never find it.

Missing Girl

This little girl of only six kept coming to me for several years. I was young at the time and really didn't know how to help her. In a high pitched voice she would tell me her killer's first name, "Steve." Then she would climb on a bike and ride it. I didn't realize Rider was the killer's last name. I had no experience and no one to turn to. I just let things be. I just kept hoping she would stop.

This has since been resolved. Sadly, she had been providing me with exactly what was needed. I had only a first name and an action. I just didn't understand how to decipher this. Eventually the killer was found and his name was Steve Rider. This made sense to me. I felt bad, this could have been resolved years ago had I known how to handle the information.

The Ghost of Bonnie

Barb came for a reading.
"Can you tell me what killed my daughter Bonnie?" Barb asked.

I closed my eyes and went to Spirit. I was shown a black spider, hanging from a thread, lowering itself onto her daughter's head.

"A poisonous spider landed in your daughter's hair and bit her."

"Did she suffer?"

"She experienced sudden flu-like symptoms and went to bed, before dying in her sleep."

"Barb, your daughter has just sent you a light pink hollow heart, which represents her love for you."

I could see Bonnie was stuck in between. I decided not to disclose this information. This would have deeply upset her mother. Later on that same evening, I helped Bonnie to cross over.

The Ghost of Betty

Betty first approached me during my sleep, in a desperate plea for help. In the dream Betty appeared monochrome. She came up to me and looked me directly in the eyes, while communicating telepathically.

"I've been dead for a year, my boyfriend Jason is a medium. He's been keeping me earthbound."

Suddenly, her eyes glazed over. Jason had snuck up behind her, grabbing the back of her neck with one hand. Then he pushed me with his other hand and sent me plummeting to the ground.

The following evening, I had closed the windows and drawn the drapes. While relaxing in the living room, I noticed the drapes moving. Next, a framed poster hanging on the wall was being disturbed. I sensed Betty's essence, but couldn't see her.

"Please leave," I requested.

After a while I went to bed and turned off the lights. While getting comfortable, I noticed Betty standing beside my bed.

"Can I help you?" I asked. "Tell me what you need."

There was no reply.

"I'm going to bed now. Perhaps we'll chat another time," I told her.
Betty vanished minutes later.

While relaxing in bed, I had forgotten to remove my delicate necklace. The pendant was of an angel encompassed in a pink heart. The clasp on this piece of jewelry was difficult to open. To remove this necklace would have taken at least five minutes. I decided to sleep with it on.

In the morning, the necklace was missing. I found it under the covers, nicely coiled beside me adjacent to my heart. I felt an odd burning sensation on my neck. Upon examining my neck in a mirror, I discovered a small round freezer burn mark, which could be the result of being touched by an entity, such as a ghost.

It was almost midnight, when Betty appeared standing in front of me. Her eyes were blinking and her skin had a bluish tone. She was in a frantic hurry to cross over and wanted my help. I called upon her spirit guides and any available angels. Within seconds, two silhouettes of winged angels appeared on either side of her. I watched the three figures approach the open golden lit doorway to the other side. Betty looked back at me, before taking her final step. Tears were in her eyes; one was running down her cheek.

"Thank you," she said to me, before turning her head and walking gracefully through the doorway with the angels.

Laura Laforce

The Ghost of Ingrid

During the middle of the day, I was preoccupied with cleaning my home. I rushed around the corner carrying my laundry basket, and encountered the ghost of a woman. A young pretty lady with blonde curly hair and blue blinking eyes stood in front of me.

Moments later my phone rang. A man, named Chris, was extremely upset and demanded to see me.

After hanging up I asked the ghost, "Are you with him?"

She responded by nodding her head up and down. This ghost went on to show me two wedding bands joined together.

"Are you his wife?"
The ghost smiled an nodded her head in agreement.

Chris arrived an hour later for his appointment. The female ghost was still present anxiously waiting to communicate with him.

"Chris, your wife is here." I started. Right away his eyes welled up with tears.

"Prove she's my wife." Chris demanded.

"The petite woman beside you is very pretty. She has curly blonde hair in a ponytail, big blue eyes and a slender face. She showed me two wedding bands before you arrived. Your wife says she is 26 years old. Her name is Ingrid and she never had a chance to say goodbye."

"Oh my God, that's her. Is she okay?" he exclaimed. "Tell her I'm sorry I went to work that day. If only I had stayed home, I could've saved her. I knew she wasn't feeling great, but I didn't know she was going to die. Did she suffer?"

Ingrid visually showed me that she passed out on the edge of the bed.

"No, she passed out and went quickly."

After 35 minutes, I could see Ingrid was ready to cross over. She lip-synched

"I love you."

"Chris, Ingrid is ready to leave to the other side. She just said I love you."

"Ingrid, I love you very much. I'm going to miss you."
Two angels were walking with her arm in arm, one on each side.

Ingrid started for the golden doorway with the Angels. She turned her head one last time, and whispered, "Thank You."

The Ghost of David

I was providing the readings for Martha's reading party. While reading Martha, two huge indigo hands appeared on the wall behind her. The fingers were spread out with a number five displayed between the hands. The prankster went on to show a large letter D, then he partially materialized. I was able to describe the youth who had appeared.

"That's David. He died in an accident, when he was only sixteen," she claimed.

"Ask him if he's responsible for switching my TV channels and turning my stereo on and off?"

David had a huge smirk on his face, while nodding his head in agreement. I understood this was how he amuses himself. It is rare to come across a ghost, who is totally enjoying himself.

After doing her reading, we started to visit.

"Laura, would you care for a snack, before your next reading arrives?" she asked.

"Sure, sounds good."

Martha had just brought the snack to the table, when David appeared. He partially materialized, sitting in between us. Martha could sense him and offered him some chips. He immediately vanished into thin air.
Fifteen minutes later, Randy arrived at Martha's for his reading. During the reading the ominous hand of David appeared against Randy's hand. He was trying to high five my client.

"Randy, a male who had passed was here to say hello."

"I never lost anybody." He replied, while glaring at me in an annoyed manner.

"David, you're not allowed to visit during this reading. My client doesn't know you."

Randy's face lit up in total amazement.
"Wait a minute!" Randy exclaimed "David was my best friend. He's welcome to stay."

"Are you sure, Randy? You just told me you hadn't lost anyone."

"David's more than welcome. Ask him if he's the one who always messing with my stereo."

David gave himself away smiling mischievously.

"Tell David he is welcome any time," he stated.

The Haunted House

Early one morning shortly after waking, I was shown a baby lying peacefully in her crib. After viewing the vision longer, I discovered she was dead. Her tiny lips were pursed together. She had dark little eyelashes. Her golden brown hair was just starting to come in. A beige blanket was pulled up to her shoulders.

An hour later, I receive a call from a man.

"Hi Laura, I don't go to psychics, but I need help."

"I recently purchased a hundred year old house. I had plans of restoring it and turning it into something nice. I didn't realize this place was haunted. Last night I woke up to see the ghost of a lady hovering directly above me. I leapt out of bed, not sure what her intentions were.

"My wife and I are on the verge of relisting the house. Is there something that can be done?"

"I could come over and find out who's there. I'm not going to guarantee the ghosts will leave."

Later that morning, I met with Gary and his wife Karen at their house.

"Gary, a male ghost is standing behind you," I said. Gary looked slightly panicked.
"Can you ask him to leave?" asked Karen.

"Not yet. I sense other entities lurking in your home. Can you show me the bedroom where most of the activities are occurring?"

Karen led the way to the upstairs bedroom. My knees were suddenly burning and felt extremely heavy, as soon as we entered the bedroom. This ghost had me by the legs.

"Let go. Let go of me now," I demanded.

I had to remind him three times before he actually let go. Upon releasing his hold on my legs, he vanished.

Minutes later, a distraught ghost of a woman appeared to me. She was looking for her baby. Many years ago her infant had died in this room.

"Go to the light, you'll find your baby on the other side," I told her.

Within seconds a bright light appeared, and she disappeared into the light.

I encountered another ghost, while leaving the room. He kept showing me the number three, followed by the number seven. I didn't understand what he was trying to tell me. Ghosts have been known to hide. He apologized for disturbing the household and chose to leave.

At seven o'clock that evening Gary called me.

"Laura, the ghost activity is ten times worse. Things are moving and banging about on the main floor. Can you come over?"

"No, I know what we're dealing with. I need a few moments."

"Can I put you on hold for a couple of minutes?"
Yes."

I closed my eyes and connected with Spirit. I was shown three ghosts that had come out of hiding. This is what the other ghost had been trying to tell me earlier.
TJ was over visiting when the call had come in.

"Look the bottom of your Christmas tree," TJ said, while pointing with excitement. "The ornament with the three wise men is spinning in circles."

TJ and I called on all angels for help. The three ghosts were refusing to move. These ghosts were rounded up and contained by the angels. They were forced into the portal, which resembles a black hole in space. A metallic looking angel sealed off the hole with a large boulder.

I took the phone off hold.

"Hi Gary, how's everything?"

"Silent and peaceful, the ghosts seem to have disappeared. Thank you."

The Ghost of Andrea

Jake hired me to clean his house, as a gift for his new wife, Maxine. While cleaning the house, things started to shift and move. I could feel an energy lurking about. The more I cleaned, the worse the activity became. I was dusting the table in the hallway when two fancy vases fell over. Thankfully, I was able to catch them. It was almost as if someone had pushed them.

Next, I started dusting in the den, when the presence became stronger. Two books randomly leapt off the shelf, landing with a thud on the hardwood floor. Minutes later, another three books came crashing down. I put down my dust cloth and stopped working.

"I understand you're upset," I said out loud. "Is there something you need to share?"

I stood waiting in the silence for a few moments before I felt a cool breeze beside me. The essence of a middle aged dark-haired woman was present.

"Can I help you?" I asked.

"My home, not hers," she said. "Who are you?"

"Andrea," she whispered.
Through telepathy she relayed, that she never felt loved. Andrea was treated with little regard during their marriage. Maxine was a friend of the family. Maxine was invading her home and husband. She put Andrea's photo away, out of sight. This bothered her the most, as she wanted to be remembered. She was stuck here due to anger and competition.

"Andrea, I will let your husband know."

After I finished cleaning the home and Jake showed up to pay me.

"Jake, Andrea is restless. She feels forgotten. She's upset that her picture has been put away," I mentioned.

"She's been dead a couple years," he snapped.

"She was ill the whole marriage. Her death was a blessing. She's in a better place." Jake failed to understand the unresolved issues.

The Museum

One evening, I brought coffee to my friend George. He was the night guard at a local museum. We had just sat down in the administration office when a blue fog randomly appeared. Seconds later, three white entities appeared, followed by an orange blur. Within minutes, I was surrounded by ten ghosts. These ghosts had successfully haunted the place for years.

I had never experienced more than two entities at a time.

"I'm only here for coffee," I said, out loud. "I'm not here to remove anybody."

"Your hair's moving – can I help?" George asked.

"George, I'm fine," I replied "These ghosts are excited and anxious to communicate."

Seconds later, a night watchman partially materialized beside me. He was dressed in a watchman uniform from the 1950's. Thirty seconds later, he vanished.

After arriving home, I was taking off my shoes. Out of the corner of my eye, I spotted a ghost.

"You're not welcome here. Go back to where you come from," I firmly stated. He disappeared and hasn't been seen since.

Séance on Radio

I arrived at the radio station to conduct a live on-air séance for a Halloween fund raiser.

The talk show hostess Mia briefly met with me before going on air.

"I don't want to sit near the board. It scares me." Mia mentioned.

"What board?" I asked.

"The Ouija board," she replied.

"I didn't bring a board. I've never used one and never will," I replied.

"You're going to do a séance without a board?" she asked.

"Yes, I don't need one to communicate with spirits," I answered.

Ten minutes later, she led me down the hall into the studio. Within minutes of being seated the show started.

"Laura, I understand you're going to conduct a séance, without a Ouija Board. Is there something the listeners should know about the Ouija Board?" she asked.

"Ouija boards are not evil, but the activity which inexperienced people conduct around them is concerning. This activity with or without a board is risky. There is always the chance of encountering dark negative spirits or opening a portal."

Mia the talk show hostess was skeptical, until she was grabbed by the wrist during the session. Other participants in the room were grabbed by the ankles.

A couple of loved ones came in to say hello or to pass on messages to different people in the room.

A prominent lady came through, wearing a purple gown. Number seventy five was repeatedly shown revealing the age she lived to. She was seventy five when she passed.

Toward the end of the séance, a couple of pranksters joined in. My hair was being pulled and lifted. After the show, I stood up and my necklace fell to the floor. I was unaware they had undone my heavy amethyst necklace.

The Hotel Ghost

We had checked into a rural hotel for the evening. On the way up to the hotel room, I could feel a presence lurking.

"Is this place haunted?" Nancy asked. "No, it's just old," Angie replied.

I decided to keep my mouth shut about the ghost. Neither of the girls would have stayed if they had known. I was exhausted I wasn't going to drive in the dark.

Shortly, after I turned out the lights, Nancy and Angie started bickering. They were accusing each other of making weird noises. Right away I could see what was happening. The ghost was riling them up.

"Ladies, let's trade places. We don't want to ruin our trip by fighting."

Moments later, loud footsteps were heard on the ceiling above us.

"Please stop," I silently asked the ghost.

In the morning, we faced a different challenge. We couldn't open the door. The room had no phone and there was no cell phone service in the area. A couple of minutes later the door was released.

The Owner

I wanted to stretch out for a short time, after checking into a motel. I looked up to discover a male ghost watching me from the foot of the bed. He was somehow attached to the property.

Before checking out of the motel the following day, I mentioned this to the owner.

"What did the ghost look like?"

"He had dark brown hair, brown eyes and fair skin."

"How old was he?"

"Around 60."

The owner went pale and took a deep breath before responding.

"That's John. He was a good friend of mine and the previous owner of this motel. He died of a heart attack."

The Settlement

We were staying at a motel in the mountains. I wasn't feeling well and found it difficult to sleep. Around three in the morning, I went to the living room. I decided to lie on the couch with the lights on.

The light had turned off, then on, off, and on with about six seconds between. My radio turned on with a fuzzy white sound.

I could hear loud footsteps, six of them to be exact, coming toward me. The sound stopped just shy of my shoulder. I looked up to see a man dressed in black pants, boots, a white shirt, and a black jacket. He was from the early 1900's.

"Mister, you're rude, is this how you treat guests?"

He suddenly vanished.

The following morning I noticed a photo directly above the sofa of an early settlement, this may have been where the hotel was built.

The Big Bang

My friend Joan came over for coffee. I could sense an entity had accompanied her. I chose to ignore it.

"Laura, my dog Muffin has been acting strange lately. Muffin keeps looking at something which isn't there. Could she being seeing a ghost?"

Out of the corner of my eye, I noticed my large picture in the hallway suddenly fly off the wall and hit the wall across from it. It landed on the hallway floor with a loud thud. We rushed over to assess the situation. The lower wall was damaged and the floor was dented by the incident.

"Joan, this ghost arrived with you earlier. I chose to ignore him. I didn't want to frighten you. This is the ghost that's been disturbing your dog."

"Is it normal for animals to see ghosts?" She asked.

"Yes, animals have souls and they're able to sense entities."

"What happens when pets die?"

"There is a heaven for animals. Their souls do go on to live. Most pets cross over immediately."

"Do animals ever become ghosts?" Joan fished.

"Any distressed soul could become a ghost," I replied.
"What happens to them?" she asked.

"The odd animal is earthbound for a very short time. These pets make brief appearances. Sometimes, they might approach you, such as rubbing up against your leg," I said.

"Have you ever had a pet visit you after dying?" Joan asked.

"Yes, when I was 14 my budgie, Feathers, died. The following morning he appeared to me, shortly after I woke up. He landed on my hand, cocked his head and looked at me. He only stayed for a few seconds before flying away," I told her.

"That's amazing. Do pets ever appear during readings?" she inquired.

"Occasionally, pets make brief appearances, but no messages are relayed."

Chapter Twenty-three

OVERWHELMED

A client called to share the birth of her son. I had originally told her the baby was female. Spirit had shown me an "F" instead of the usual pink or blue. I remember during her reading, she was concerned about the swine flu and the new baby. The letter "F" meant fine, not female. I was accurate on his birth weight of eight pounds seven ounces.

An hour later, Neil arrived for a reading. He was trying to deal with his father's earthbound spirit. Toward the end of his reading, he pulled out a photo of his dead father in a coffin.

"Is this the ghost you're seeing?" he asked.

"Yes."

Later that afternoon, I seriously questioned my ability to help others. Understanding things correctly is important to me. I take things seriously when working with others. While growing up I always wanted to be a mother and a baker. I never planned on being a psychic medium.

I decided to take care of some housework for awhile. After stripping my bed the mattress was bare. I returned to my room with clean sheets to discover something on the bed. I notice an object on my bed, which at a distance looked like a small piece of wood. Upon closer examination it was a leather label which read, "Almost Famous."
This "Almost Famous" was a message from Spirit. I didn't even want to participate any more. I was down from the events earlier in the day. This was really starting to take a hit on my pride. Ego can't serve Spirit. I needed to come to this realization for growth.

The Return

Earlier in the day, I was attending a meeting. While sharing psychic experiences, I suddenly became ill. My entire abdomen bloated three times its size and jumped with spasms. I was in so much pain my legs were shaking.

Suddenly people in the room were feeling my pain and sickness.

Marc, the medicine man started to assist me. Marc immediately went to the rock display. He picked the rock his spirit guide had shown him and handed it to me.

"Put this rock on your stomach, where it hurts the most."

This rock immediately absorbed half the pain and cracked in two places. Marc stood beside me, with his hands ready for healing. He quietly asked Spirit why I was sick and how to help.

"Laura, close your eyes. I need you to focus on what I'm being shown. A very sick and twisted entity is holding onto you. This entity appears like a twisted spine of a snake. It has a hold of your whole abdomen."

I closed my eyes, the twisted entity, morphed into Paul, the medium that I dated before I met TJ. He was crying with his mouth wide open, like a young child in a temper tantrum.

"Oh my God. It's Paul."

"Tell this entity the contract is over. Tell him you want a divorce." Marc declared.

"I'm not married. I only dated him for six months." I replied.

"Perhaps this is a past life contract you have with him. He needs to understand this is over."

233

This was the worst psychic attack I had experienced. Prior to this attack there were other mild attacks. A heavy feeling in the solar plexus or a sudden headache would manifest after seeing an apparition of Paul.

Once I spotted a black eagle fly across the living room, which morphed into a blob of dark energy. Attached to this energy were intense feelings of sadness. The following night, an image of a black crow flew past my peripheral line of vision. It headed straight out my office window.

Unusual things started to happen. I become sad and irritated in regard to my relationship with TJ, but nothing was wrong. We both experienced sudden overwhelming feelings of sadness about our upcoming wedding. These feelings were completely unfounded.

Shortly after returning home from the meeting, I headed to bed. I was feeling drained from being psychically attacked at the meeting.

Hours later, I awoke. While lying awake, I started experiencing cold feet about our upcoming wedding. TJ is my best friend, our love had stemmed from a strong friendship. Why was I feeling like this?

Many questions were rapidly running through my head. Was everything really going to be okay? What sort of changes would marriage bring? Would boredom set in due to being so similar? These thoughts had come on so sudden and strong.

While mulling through my thoughts, there was a sudden loud thud in my walk-in closet. I jumped out of bed to investigate. The box containing my headpiece for our wedding was in the middle of the floor. I knew Paul was behind this. I quickly surrounded myself by light. "Spirit, protect me," I silently called out.

The Flag

Shortly after climbing back into bed, Spirit started downloading me with information for the following day. I had been quietly observing the black and white slide show of people's faces, hands and situations. This lasted almost fifteen minutes.

Toward the end, a race track flag with three stripes was revealed. One silk royal blue stripe was between two white canvas stripes. An unfamiliar female's voice interrupted, powerfully commanding,

"Love" "Endure" "Evolve"

I didn't understand and became very concerned. These were our wedding colors. Was the flag a warning? I lay awake the most the night, trying to comprehend this.
The flag was not red, I reasoned. They use flags at the races to count down events. Three more big events were to happen, including our wedding day, I reasoned. What about the love though? This scared me. Was something wrong, I wondered?

The next day before starting my readings, I mentioned this to Marc the medicine man while having coffee.

"Ask your spirit guides to repeat themselves. They're probably trying to tell you something about TJ, which you need to know in order to make this relationship work," Marc said.

"This voice was unfamiliar, it wasn't my guides," I replied in frustration.

I waited until evening and called Charlene, an acquaintance of mine, who was a medium herself.

"Laura, you've got cold feet. Don't worry, many brides get jittery before their weddings. It's normal. It was probably your own thoughts in your head you heard. Remember when saying your vows, the answer is 'I do'. Your old mantra,

235

'I'm not ready yet', no longer suits you."

I thanked Charlene and hung up the phone, still very leery. I felt panicked and upset. Our wedding was only three weeks away. What was I going to do?

I decided to call TJ and share this with him.

"Laura, try not to worry. If something was wrong, we would both be shown. I have no bad feelings about this message or our wedding," TJ replied trying to reassure me.

After hanging up the phone, I went to Spirit.

"Please help me with this?" I begged while panicking.

I started reflecting on all the past visions of us. I was shown TJ, years before I met him. Spirit revealed events which we would share. Some of these visions had already passed. Why was I suddenly experiencing cold feet? What was I scared of?

I spent most of the evening deep in thought, searching my soul. Hours later, I discovered my fear. Over the past several years, I went home alone. Nobody was behind closed doors hurting me. For the first time in my entire life, I was safe, happy, at peace and secure. I valued this. Recognizing and acknowledging these feelings, put my cold feet at ease.

Intuition Ignored

The following evening, three weeks before the wedding. I was spending time with Kate.

"Laura, I brought us some soy parfaits for dessert. Would you like to try one?"

"Are you sure you want to try this?" my intuition warned.

"I'll try a teaspoon of yours," I replied.

Seconds later my tongue was burning, within minutes hives erupted. Hours later, I was covered in hives, from head to toe. This was a severe allergy, which could have been life threatening. I was ill for weeks.

New hives were still emerging the day before the wedding. I wondered how I was going to wear my beautiful gown. Had I listened to and respected my intuition, this would have never happened.

The wedding party gathered for a rehearsal, the night before our wedding. While we were practicing our entrance, a friend was taking pictures. One of the finished photos picked up TJ's mother's orb.

Our Wedding

In the early hours of the morning, I woke hearing drops of rain on the roof.

"Dan you showed me good weather for our wedding. Please don't let our special day be rainy," I begged.

Dan sent a flash of yellow, letting me know everything was going to be fine. I gradually drifted back to sleep.

Upon waking in the morning, the sun was shining through the curtains. I was up early with excitement, anticipating the day. I felt better. The welts were now under control and starting to subside. This was the day I would marry TJ, my soul mate, the man intended for me.

I wore a beautiful designer wedding gown and a feathered headpiece with crystals woven into my hairstyle. I looked identical to the bride revealed to me in a vision.

Moments before walking down the aisle, I became overwhelmed. Visions I had seen over the years were rapidly unfolding, one at a time. The marriage commissioner was late and excused himself as he rushed by me. His face, clothing, and the book

237

he was carried were identical.

The bridal party had already walked down the aisle. Now it was my turn. I entered smiling and walking gracefully. TJ was standing at the front, smiling as he waited for me.

My face started to jump and twitch out of control during my entrance. TJ met me at the front and offered his warm loving hand. He whispered something nice to me, as we walked hand in hand to the arch.

We stood face to face, holding hands, while exchanging our vows. TJ was the handsome gentle man, dressed in the tuxedo, which Spirit revealed to me. I stood looking into his loving brown eyes. His face started to twitch, the same as mine. Everything was so touching, I started to cry. TJ gently massaged my hands in a loving calming manner.

While heading to the signing table, the wall, and the floor became extremely familiar. After we signed the registry, another vision started to unfold. The vision previously revealed the bride being a little teary, slightly overwhelmed, but very happy.

We strolled down the aisle hand in hand, together at last.

"I'm the luckiest man on earth. I love you."

Speeches were made in front of a white canvas and silk royal blue backdrop. TJ's four sisters gave a beautiful presentation. Right after their speech, his eldest sister, whom I had never met before, firmly commanded out loud at the end of her speech:

"Love" "Endure" "Evolve"

TJ and I enjoyed our wedding with all our lovely guests. Before midnight we headed off to our honeymoon suite. We spent a romantic evening together, reminiscing about our day. I awoke in the early morning hours. Spirit presented two flashcards, with words printed in golden block sized capital letters.

ABOUT THE AUTHOR

I was born in Edmonton, Alberta, into a devout Catholic family. I was a different child, considered to have severe learning disabilities.

At four years old, I could astral travel through the walls at night. While awake, I was clumsy and uncoordinated, constantly walking into things, almost as if my physical body didn't have boundaries. Around eight years old, I could see both good and bad future events, including the death of my best friend.

My childhood and teenage years were full of turmoil and challenges. I never understood what I was dealing with until much later. Many times, I wanted this weirdness to stop. I even tried to shut it down. My gift went unrecognized until I was almost an adult. Eventually I learned how to work with my abilities on my own.

I struggled with my gift for many years, up to the age of thirty two. While attending a family reunion, I came across interesting historical information. I have royal blood in my genes, and the family had a secret they referred to as "the curse". After talking with extended relations and putting the pieces together, my abilities finally made sense.

Today I work as an intuitive, clairvoyant and spiritualist helping others. I teach others how to develop their abilities through workshops and lectures.

- Laura Laforce

Read about this story and more in Book Two

' X-tending'

Laura Laforce

Manor House
905-648-2193
www.manor-house.biz